Neil M. Denari
Gyroscopic Horizons

 Thames & Hudson

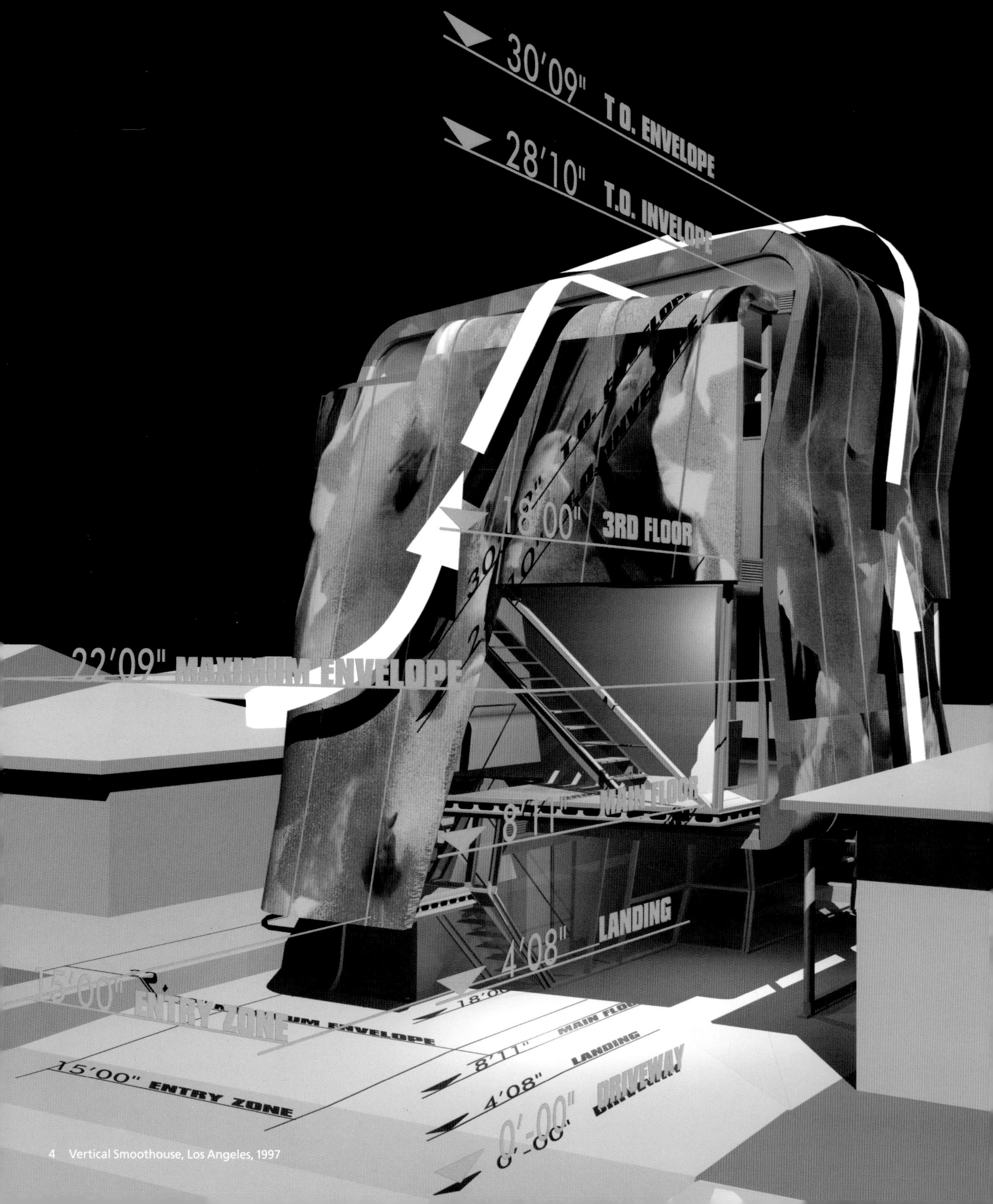

30'09" T.O. ENVELOPE

28'10" T.O. INVELOPE

18'00" 3RD FLOOR

22'09" MAXIMUM ENVELOPE

8'0" MAIN FLOOR

4'08" LANDING

15'00" ENTRY ZONE

18'00"

8'11" MAIN FLOOR

4'08" LANDING

0'-00" DRIVEWAY

15'00" ENTRY ZONE

0'-00"

Contents

Acknowledgments

Gyroscopic Horizons has had a long gestation period—a number of years, in fact. While the work has grown in its exploration and focus, the publishers and editors at Princeton Architectural Press have remained committed to its eventuation. I must thank Kevin Lippert for his support of this work and Clare Jacobson for her careful editing and project management. In London, Lucas Dietrich of Thames and Hudson has been a catalyzing influence on the book.

In various large cities around the world, Aaron Betsky, Herbert Muschamp, Henry Urbach, Terence Riley, Yuki Fuchigami, and Philip Uzzan have been generous and supportive of the work.

In Texas, Edward Baum and Joan Davidow have been open and engaging colleagues.

In New York, thanks go to Taeg Nishimoto, Marc Rosenbaum, and Laurence Turner for their continuing friendship.

In Japan, I am grateful to Yasuyuki Okazaki, Masao Yahagi, Kiyokazu Arai, Tadashi Murai, Kei'ichi Irie, Sei'ichi Kozu, and Riichi Miyake, and especially to Masaaki Oka, for his dedication to the work and ideas of the office, and to Noriko Oka, for her help, hospitality, and good cheer.

In London, my conversations with Peter Cook, Yael Riesner, and Christine Hawley, among many others at the Bartlett, have always been convivial and inspiring.

In Portland, I have learned from Whitney Lowe through his collaborative enthusiasm.

In Los Angeles, the faculty, students, and staff at SCI-Arc, as well as my predecessors there, Ray Kappe and Michael Rotondi, must be thanked for creating a lively critical atmosphere in which to teach and work. It is an extraordinary school of which I am proud to be a part.

Also in Los Angeles, Andrew Waisler, Benny Chan, Wyndham Chow, and, in particular, Tomoharu Ono, all SCI-Arc graduates, have been instrumental in the life and production of the work in the book. My research assistants, Rebecca Rudolph and Christopher Pfiffner, should be thanked for their valuable work which has greatly informed the content of this book.

I am indebted to Peter Zellner for his critical reading of the text and for his contagious enthusiasm for architectural debate.

This book would not have emerged without the information, interest, dedication, and humor of Richard Massey. Our ongoing conversations led to many ideas presented here. My thanks to him for this and for capturing the spirit of my work. His partner, Miko McGinty, should also be thanked for her important work on the book in the form of critical design assistance and production and project management.

My deepest gratitude goes to my wife, Christine. Her unyielding support and understanding of these endeavors, along with her critical feedback, has been extraordinary. This book simply would not exist without her.

Finally, this book is dedicated to my parents, Edward and Muriel Denari. Their lives and energy course through every page.

Desire x Ingenuity

Since 1960, the North American landscape, especially the Southwestern part of the United States, has undergone massive development due to the expansion of the military-industrial complex that served the space program and the sustained conflict in Vietnam. The economies of extraction and material fabrication later merged with the "clean" industries of computer manufacturing and other information-related operations that accelerated in the early 1970s. During the last quarter-century, forms of urbanization that emphasize the *terrain vague* of horizontal conditions have mirrored the decentralized structures of information industries. My home region, the Dallas–Fort Worth area, is known as the Metroplex, a word invented to describe the phenomenon of the complex metropolitan environment. This region exemplifies how the technological landscapes of this time have come to embody the late-twentieth-century concept of what J.G. Ballard has called the unlimited possibility: *desire x ingenuity = America*. This is the cultural and physical landscape that forms the basis of my own developing identity. It is at once global in its implications and specific in its milieu.

From 1983 to 1992, my work argued for relevance via an autobiographical positioning of ideas. Since 1992, my interest has shifted from the narrowly focused machine reference to the broad and open possibilities of cultural conditions not yet coded with an architectural symbol. In the struggle to outline ideas that are architecturally relevant—those ideas presented in this book—I have recognized that a continuous series of cross sections must be cut through the global cultural structures that have come to dominate our contemporary lives so that the progress, ambivalence, possibilities, and shifts recorded in theses slices may inform my work. Indeed, if there is a self-consciousness to this work, it is based on movement—that

its plane of consistency is not secretly a box that limits. In cinema, even when Yasujiro Ozu's camera (a device we could call a limited box) doesn't move, the images multiply, a feeling is generated. As Gilles Deleuze writes, "But this is not what is important, because a movement may also be exaggerated, be incessant, become a world-movement, a Brownian movement, a trampling, a to-and-fro, a multiplicity of movements on different scales. What is important is that the anomalies of movement become the essential point instead of being accidental or contingent."

Sections

Since the early 1990s, I have begun to understand how the popularity of technoscientific discourse and application has sponsored issues ranging from the crises of identity loss (due to homogenization) to the production of new and emergent cultural groups found in digital fields. It is impossible, therefore, for me to conceive of a relevant discourse in architecture that does not argue its presence through the pathways of culture. Here, culture has two forms. One is an apparition, like quicksand, a mirage, or a blob, offering us an image that shifts, disappears, or changes its shape instantly. Like a drunk walking in an earthquake, sometimes we do not notice the undulation of movement. The second form is a ferocious beast, consuming us at every turn. These twin phenomena of culture have come to mirror the logic of my work, which is built on the idea that the ambivalent fields of repetitive and processed spaces and the traditional desire to produce difference (the expressive *auteur*) exist together as a productive cultural condition. It acknowledges the forces (fatal, hegemonic, or otherwise) that coordinate to both limit and open up the possible ways in which architecture can become simultaneously an extrapolator *and* a producer of culture.

Architecture has its most impressive effect when it is understood as a material discourse. Not to continue the project of building as merely the restatement of the real, this effectiveness asserts the idea that architecture is *the* experimental medium. Unlike cinema, which filmmaker Hollis Frampton has called the last machine, architecture is always the first.

The Minor

Deleuze reminds us not about limits but rather illusion or even self-deception when he writes: *A philosophical concept can never be confused with a scientific function or an artistic construction, but finds itself in affinity with these in this or that domain of science or style of art. The scientific or artistic content of a philosophy may be very elementary, since it is not obliged to advance art or science, but it can advance itself only by forming properly philosophical concepts from a given function or construction, however elementary.*[4]

The first eight parts of this book are elementary, if not essential. They form a minor landscape of words and images that assert a (minor) world. In the end, on every page, there is only architecture here, that medium which I am obliged to advance. And still closer to the end, which is really just a point of becoming, Jean-Luc Godard's famous phrase, *"Pas une image juste, juste une image"* (not a just image, just an image) comes to mind, and again, so does Deleuze, who says in reference to Godard's phrase, "Well, but ideas—having an idea—isn't ideology, it's practice."[5]

This book is about ideas. Not correct ideas or owned ideas or my ideas. It is about styles, practices—minor movements.

[1] The complex, disarticulated physical environment of the Metroplex could not be objectified or understood except symbolically through the forms of its own material production, primarily that of the aerospace industry. During the 1960s and 1970s, my father was an engineer on the team developing VSTOL aircraft and, later, helicopters for civilian use. Airports, hotel slabs, hangars, industrial installations—these were my first impressions of modernist architecture. Along with the astonishing forms of the aircraft themselves, this architecture seemed to be *mine*. The exposure to this level of animated industrial technology was the basis for an autobiographically stated architectural position I held later on. The work used technological expression as a code for both the personal, authentic, and machinic aspects of its production.

[2] Gilles Deleuze, *Cinema 2: The Time-Image*, trans. Hugh Tomlinson and Robert Galeta (Minneapolis: University of Minnesota Press, 1989), 128.

[3] "The task of life is to make all these repetitions coexist in a space in which difference is distributed." Gilles Deleuze, *Difference and Repetition*, trans. Paul Patton (New York: Columbia University Press, 1994), xix.

[4] Ibid., xii.

[5] Gilles Deleuze, "Interview: Three Questions about 'Six Fois Deux,'" *Son + Image* (New York: Museum of Modern Art, 1992), 35.

The book begins with the idea that there is no place to start. With no origin, it is not a monograph but a *multigraph*: a merger of textforms, onirosigns,[1] and architecture. This is a book that begins midway. It presumes that other books have been written but not published, projects designed but not exposed. It is written by a single person passing through many plenums, engaging with others in the world, conspiring with the legions of people whose energy and ideas *make* the world—a world where Godard speaks to Zapruder and the mechanical and the fluid are engaged in a lovers' discourse.

The world in this book is both a painfully limited and an unremittingly extended construction, formed by the anxious mixture of persuasion, inevitability, and doubt—indeed, a twentieth-century cocktail served by the agents of desire. In the airport departure lounge, a gate is simply a coupling device, joining two different pathways at a physical point of osculation.[2] Flights always involve at least two gates, so neither one is *the* gate in the system of all possible gates. Moreover, as an osmotic membrane,[3] the transit lounge/gate equalizes the flows of different lines of flight, allowing the human to enter into a global space of physical transition. This is only the most obvious structure to ask the book to model itself after. With a world of possibilities in mind, the work in this book moves toward the question of place with the same dynamic flow as a Boeing crossing the international dateline[4] headed for the arrival lounge at Tokyo's Narita Airport.

Starting is always occupying the everpresent now. The departure lounge is an architectural reference for a place that is not a destination but a moment (even if it is hours) within a continuous trajectory or process of movement.

¹ An image where a movement of world replaces action. Gilles Deleuze, *Cinema 2: The Time-Image*, trans. Hugh Tomlinson and Robert Galeta (Minneapolis: Minnesota University Press, 1989), 335.

² Cf. "Osculations," 43.

³ A flexible surface made up of a semipermeable material where fluids move through to equalize levels of concentration on either side of the surface. It should be noted here, near the outset of this book, that a relation will be cast between models of thinking that are impossibly pliant and ones that are sturdy, because would it be possible today to describe certain architectural propositions without the lush and open-ended (technical) language of the life sciences? It seems that almost no architect is completely immune to the models offered by the soft systems of molecular biology, especially as they are transposed through forms of communication (media-based languages, etc.) that are themselves compounding the possible theoretical positions for architecture. The works in this book, while less indebted to the formal models of biological systems, do nonetheless employ the conceptual and abstract terminologies of such systems. After more than a decade (who can really know how long?) of rapid absorption into the discourse of architecture, concepts and fields such as entropy, cybernetics, self-organizing systems, neural networks, and complexity have helped construct new formations of meaning, geometry, and space.

⁴ Approximately following the 180th meridian, the international dateline (ID) marks a line separating the East and the West by a calendar day. Moving through the Bering Strait in the north, the ID separates Wake Island, the Marshall Islands, and Fiji in the east from Midway, Hawaii, the Aleutian Islands, and Samoa in the west. It is sixteen or seventeen hours (depending on Daylight Savings Time) *later* in Tokyo than Los Angeles.

Additionally, if one were to stand on the ID facing north, Japan would be to the west and Los Angeles to the east, thus inverting or shifting to the center of the Pacific Ocean the line between east and west. Would this mean that Los Angeles is no longer the Occident but the new Orient?

Gyroscopic Horizon[1]

An artificial horizon line. A diagram of the fixed ground superimposed on the fluctuating conditions of both controlled and impulsive movement. In flight, it allows a pilot to understand the relation (pitch and roll) of the airplane to the *real* horizon line.[2] This book takes as its title the name of the device that does *not* describe the plan or terrestrial position of the airplane but rather indicates the equilibrium or orientation of the plane within the sectional flow of its movement through open air space. Thinking of the world as an infinite series of plenums where all matter and phenomena move with a limitless spectrum of directions, speeds, and destinations suggests that architecture is a practice that locates itself through vision (the scopic territory). Although buildings occupy ground, perhaps the strategies of their making arise out of the registration of, at a particular place and moment in time, a multiple number of horizontal pathways. As we move across, below, through, and above the horizon lines of fields, cities, and skies, the sediment of experience includes the layers of multiple in-between movements, not just the beginnings and the ends. Real or banal, imagined or cosmic, there is always the "horizon of events," as Michelangelo Antonioni has said, which here may be interpreted as a multiplying of horizons.[3]

Indeed, within the constant flow and movement of technology, politics, and economics, it is necessary to find orientation without the fixity of place.[4] However, if every day is a new context, how will we know where we are in ways that a global positioning system (GPS) device cannot tell us? When is awareness of the ground no longer the primary referent in explaining the complexity of the momentary conditions of the everpresent? Is it possible that architecture can mutate into equal parts GPS, abstract machine, event horizon, and vague placeform, a kind of quadfurcation[5] of the purpose of building?

Architecture is an artificial landscape responding to fluctuating conditions, deploying supple forms and programs that have the potential to elude the restrictions of its own universe of doubt, that it is too big, too heavy, and too mute to accurately describe or produce our world.

¹ *Gyro*, from the Greek, means circle or spiral. It conspires with *scopic* to produce a word meaning sighting the circle.

² Horizon: the persistent moment in space and time where land and sky meet, which no matter what the elevation above sea level is always at eye level, except for astronauts. Even at 35,000 ft. (6.62 mi./10.72 km), the curvature of the earth is not perceptible; it seems horizontal, reiterating the *y* axis in the Cartesian cruciform of *x, y,* and *z*.

Boeing/Collins have developed new instrumentation through computer graphic displays called EADI (electronic attitude-director indicator) and EHSI (electronic horizontal-situation indicator). The EHSI provides a color display of the plan location of the plane. The interesting thing to note here is the term *horizontal situation*. It approximates the terms *horizontal cut* or *slice*, which architects sometimes use to describe a plan view.

³ Gilles Deleuze recalls Antonioni's view of the twofold meaning of horizon in the West as both ordinary and cosmic. He cites European humanism (ordinary) and U.S. science fiction (cosmic) as genres of cinema that describe each condition. Japan, contrarily, is not concerned with a bifurcation of the horizon into a dualist cinematic discourse. There, a single horizon links all levels of human drama. *Cinema 2: The Time Image* (Minneapolis: University of Minnesota Press, 1989), 17. A multiplication of horizons, however, describes a new perception of a real-time Cartesian world. With computer technology, *x, y,* and *z* simply organize a field in which spatial conditions may be viewed from points in the field and therefore are not ballasted along any specific axis of viewing or denotation.

⁴ With the developments in the 1930s of Heisenberg's uncertainty principle and Gödel's theory of incompleteness, the studies of determining the location and logic of physical and mathematical systems reached an ironic form of conclusiveness: that there is no finite and controllable end to either the dynamics of trajectories/events or in the ruthless formality of an apparently finite set of formulae. From these rather dramatic shifts in knowledge came the two most charged leitmotifs in science (and culture) of the last sixty years: the concepts of *potential* and *doubt*, otherwise called *the unknown*. Seemingly dialectical, one is the embodiment of *becoming*, the other a signal of failure in the rational discourse. More importantly, however, both embody the infinite in the endless tracking of occurrences and perturbations within organized systems. Breakdowns herald new possibilities, while movements that cannot be charted ceaselessly follow continuously changing courses.

⁵ Bifurcation x 2.

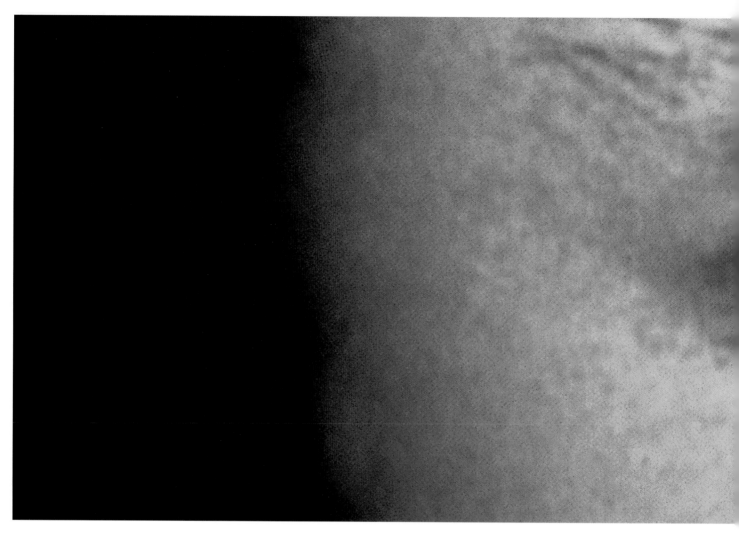

Space Is the Place

In no other time has the concept, meaning, and logic of place been studied with equal parts suspicion and vigilance; for indeed, the contemporary world seems to reject any attempt (by architects, politicians, filmmakers, or anyone else who dares to create strategies for organizing phenomena) to design the precise parameters of place. If only by the excessive distortions in time and distance wrought by the digital world, the intricate relation of these phenomena to place has changed forever the ways in which we map ourselves in a global world.[1] In fact, not simply as a resistance mechanism or an antidote to the hyperplacelessness of urban and economic fields (the market*place*), architecture, quite often the culprit in the banal (at least in America!), now has the chance to uproot itself from its own implosive gravity to perform in new ways.

From Heidegger's concept of clearing out for the placeform to Samuel Butler's inverted novel of nowhere, *Erewhon*,[2] (the here and the now fashioned out of placelessness), from the Ryoan-ji Zen Garden in Kyoto to the Farnsworth House, place is never a singular idea leading to a concrete liminality. Bounded physical space is now utterly compromised by mobility, technology, the fluctuation of borders, and the heterogeneity of cultures—so much so that architecture must conspire with the complex forces at work in the resolution of placements. But what are these forces? What will result from the speculative accumulation of them for architecture? And what are the strategies that can be developed to contend with forces that seem to be more immediate, fluxual, and overwhelming in effect? Today architecture is not about clearing out, it is about a lack of fitting in.

Mobile Identities

Questions of the loss of identity, of authenticity, of coherence in our world are dramatized, however, by the rhetoric of the media or even of complex forms in architecture itself that seek to symbolize the profound changes in our reading of the concept of place. In referring to the media as a gigantic machine of hyperbolized banality, Gianni Vattimo writes, "Indeed, everything sent out by the mass media is imbued with a strange air of fragility and superficiality."[3] In contrast to the stability, eternity, and authenticity of previous regimes of aesthetic production, Vattimo argues, there are, in the face of apparent standardizing aspects of global forces, new responses to the emotions of loss. "Perhaps we have now reached the stage where we can recognize that the superficiality and fragility of aesthetic experience in late modern society do not necessarily have to be signs and symptoms of alienation linked to the dehumanizing aspects of standardization.... [I]t is also the society in which reality presents itself as *softer* and *more fluid*, and in which experience can again acquire the characteristics of oscillation, disorientation, and play [*italics mine*]."[4] After all, the desire to defend specific forms or cultural identities against globally hegemonic forces like the media or the corporate world has within it the potential for an unconscious modus operandi of ghettoization and self-imposed oppression. Movements cannot occur, therefore, if resistance is based on nostalgia. Hegemony, in fact, for Ernesto Laclau and Chantal Mouffe, is an open-ended and temporal phenomenon that is simply a provisional stabilizing of identities that are otherwise always on the move, highly fluid. Laclau and Mouffe argue that an inert identity is not possible, as every identity is forged from multiple sources of culture and history. For every subject, there is a story. Everyone is an enigma—with an inherent genealogy of differences.[5]

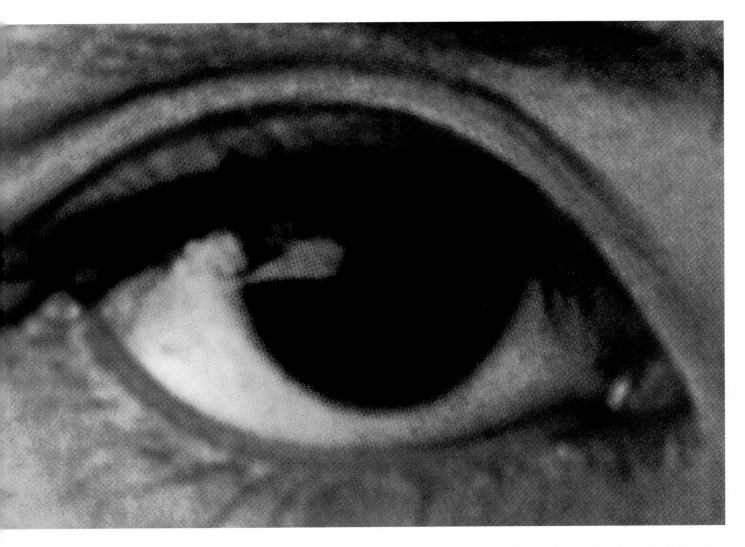

Question: Not how to de-dramatize these hyperboles and potential failures, but how to deal with them directly, productively?[6]

(/) Symbol for *Between*

Global form and the production of repetitive space is a process of adding to the conditions of specific form; thus it is not about incurring loss of either space or identity but the production of a variety of spaces. Understanding the relations between *placelessness* and *place without limit* allows a coherent architectural proposition to emerge from contemporary phenomena. Specific performances (the here and now) and abstract/symbolic codes merge (with the here and there).

[1] Fredric Jameson, "Postmodernism and Consumer Society," in *The Cultural Turn* (New York: Verso, 1998), 15. See also Michael Speaks, "From the Foundational Postmodern to the Immanent Modern: Reading Jameson Reading Architecture," in *The Critical Landscape* (Rotterdam: 010 Publishers), 58.

[2] Gilles Deleuze refers to *Erewhon* in his opening remarks in *Difference and Repetition*, trans. Paul Patton (New York: Columbia University Press, 1994), 21.

[3] Gianni Vattimo, *The Transparent Society* (Baltimore: Johns Hopkins University Press, 1992), 57.

[4] Ibid., 59.

[5] See Ernesto Laclau and Chantal Mouffe, *Hegemony and Socialist Strategy: Towards a Radical Democratic Politics* (New York: Verso, 1989).

[6] "But modern thought is born of the failure of representation, of the loss of identities, and of the discovery of all the forces that act under the representation of the identical." Deleuze, *Difference and Repetition*, 19.

The basic conditions indispensable to the projects here: build space within the world of systems with materials, color codes, and escalations.

What does it mean to build today, in a world where structures and organizations of all kinds collapse under the avalanche of the now as quickly as they are thought? Of course I am not speaking only of architecture but also of every other system operating today. The callousness of capital, the quicksilver logic of trend, the mobility of the masses, the entropy and flow of energies—does one dare to entertain, in this arena of hyperfragility, a discourse on *firmitas* without consciously arguing that the heaviness of architecture is not an impediment in resolving forces? Should there be laughter among those who have abandoned building or among those who were never condemned to craft space, at the hopes and dreams of the ones who desperately welcome such condemnation?

At the outset, an architecture motivated by the contemporaneity of events in the world (realism) is guided by the will to apply rather than to abstract knowledge. This desire to manifest is in response to the reassessments of knowledge now going on in many disciplines. Francisco Varela writes, "At the very center of this emerging view is the belief that the proper units of knowledge are primarily *concrete, embodied, incorporated, lived.*"[1] Application involves the reifying of knowledge into a *usable* and/or readable state, one where the sensations of the material space provide an ineffable feeling.[2] The usable state, no doubt, refers to the implementation of effects within a building that are receptive to the engagement of the body. Historically, architecture has concretized knowledge by its ability to convey a certain programmed function-state; it coheres when it represents a condition of use through its spatial domain. Does building reach its mastery of reality when its objectification by design houses a smoothly operating system of humans with intent to do something?

[1] Francisco Varela, "The Reenchantment of the Concrete," *Zone 6: Incorporations* (New York: Zone Books, 1992), 320.

[2] "Such sensations do not act as metaphors, transferring us to other objects or images serving as points of reference. The material and its durability are what support and produce both the perceptions we receive by means of our senses and the effects that are neither merely subjective nor to be considered pure reactions on the part of the individual confronted with the work." Ignasi de Solà-Morales, *Differences*, trans. Graham Thompson, ed. Sarah Whiting (Cambridge, MA: MIT Press, 1996), 33.

Systems

What is meant by a system? Virtually all conditions in the world operate via systems that organize and structure a comprehensive assemblage of equipment (artificial or natural) and information.

Organizational system, design system, political system, structural system, modular system, corporate system, credit system, biological system, mechanical system, electrical system, circulation system, sign system—the complexity of these human-physical systems is generated from the buildup of micro-events and actions. Through systems analysis, any object, process, act, or idea may be connected to a system. Above all, systems are seen to have functions and economies, even if they are not driven by utilitarian needs.

How is a system different from a structure? If structure is defined as the set of relations connecting the elements of a system, then it follows that systems are related elements waiting to be structured.

Objects

The object may be evaluated via four logics of signification, as utilized by Jean Baudrillard:
— *A functional logic of use value*
— *An economic logic of exchange value*
— *A logic of symbolic exchange*
— *A logic of sign value*
The first is a logic of practical operations; the second, one of equivalence; the third, ambivalence; and the fourth, difference. Or again: a logic of utility, a logic of the market, a logic of the gift, and a logic of status. Organized in accordance with one of the above groupings, the object assumes respectively the status of an *instrument*, a *commodity*, a *symbol*, or a *sign.*[1]

Baudrillard distinguishes the sign value from the material value of an object through difference. As commodities are consumed, they become signs of another system beyond the utilitarian. Accordingly, an object generates meaning in an abstract value system relative to all other object-signs. It is only when seen against all other objects in the commercial field that any object may be understood to be part of a system. Roland Barthes reiterates this when he says that given a society, all objects will automatically become signs. This is perhaps the moment when the rhetoric of functionalist modern landscapes, buildings, and interiors became suspect. Baudrillard breaks down the one-dimensional nature of function as utilitarian when he writes: *The term evokes all the virtues of modernity, yet it is perfectly ambiguous. With its reference to "function" it suggests that the object fulfills itself in the precision of its relationship to the real world and to human needs. But as our analysis has shown,* functional in no way qualifies what is adapted to a goal, merely what is adapted to an order or system: *functionality is the ability to become integrated into an overall scheme.*[2]

Buildings

Buildings, apart from people and nature, constitute the material and spatial density of the city. They make a nature and, like objects, they can be classified. Would it be strange, despite the everpresence of building, to consider architecture as part of our consumer society, that realm where objects are the vessels of unbelievable desire? Due to a cost commensurate with size (if not always quality), architecture is a commodity for a few, a necessity for most, and potentially desired by all. Indeed, all the houses and high-rises in the world cannot add up to the number of products occupying the ever-thickening, highly impastoed world of commercial artifacts. Architecture, therefore, is consumed not in a point-of-purchase scenario but as space, as style, as its own system of objects.

Response to Baudrillard's four logics:
— *Buildings appear because of use. They house something called a* program, *a precise or vague set of the users' spatial needs.*
— *Speculators and users who develop or own buildings regard them as assets. Every floor plate is a miniature economy in itself, a commodity in a world of finite building sites.*[3]
— *How does architecture generate value beyond its utilitarian or market value? How else can it function such that an actual value can be ascertained, if not quantified?*[4] *Public buildings such as museums are usually understood as symbols in the city—those institutions offering images, ideas, and artifacts to the knowledge-consuming public.*
— *Conventional wisdom suggests that form or aesthetics in objects may codify the sign value of architecture—that is, a box may be a signform for straightforwardness, an ascetic or sober response to its use value, or an eccentrically shaped building may be a signform for progress, delight, or the signature of the* auteur *(brand name?).*

Umberto Eco offers a second analysis of sign functions, patterned after Hjelmslev.[5] The four levels are already installed in relation to architecture:
— *Expression-substance:* the total of all possibilities that can articulate space and matter.
— *Expression-form:* the system of architectonic oppositions and thus structures of form.
— *Content-substance:* all possible architectural functions in a given culture.
— *Content-form*: the system of meanings that a culture associates with architecture.[6]

To assert that architecture is a conjunction of expressions and forms is obvious. But what should architecture express other than its own internal logic? Is the moment when content becomes expression, surely an accurate if schematic view of functionalist architecture, the moment when buildings exert the most pleasure,[7] the most rightness? As content here is a splicing of use and systems of meanings, architecture can only become pleasurable when its idiomorphic aspects become readable and culturally relevant and thus not simply offered on the credit of the progress card we are so often tempted to use.

To move from the analysis of objects through Baudrillard to a semiotics/language-referenced analysis suggests that architecture is never far from the sign of its own making.

What constitutes the architectural world system? It could be asked, when related to the biological model, if architecture must now always be an open and dynamic system, rejecting completely the near equilibrium of the static or closed system? After all, if architecture has undergone radically positive conceptual transformations via the biological model of systems, will it ever, as a discipline, be able to refer to equilibrium or the fixed again? It will not, even if buildings *appear* otherwise.

[1] Jean Baudrillard, *For a Critique of the Political Economy of the Sign* (n.p., Telos Press, 1981), 66.

[2] Jean Baudrillard, *The System of Objects* (New York: Verso, 1996), 63. It is not within the present scope to furnish an analysis of modernist architecture other than to say that my work is itself structured around modernist principles both of function and the exploitation of material and structural possibilities available today. When curtain walls, cantilevers, free spatial division, and sheer abstraction of geometry are involved, the work is considered structured by but not limited to the fixed and totalizing tenants of the modern. Indeed, the use of modern strategies is unavoidable today, except where design processes involve instrumentalizing responses to program. The impossibility of "shrink-wrapping" use is only the first criticism in the move toward a more flexible formal outcome informed by the plethora of forces at work on a building. My practice is based on the fusion of pragmatics of research *and* the recognition of the cultural project of difference.

As a design field, especially in the Era of Good Design (Charles and Ray Eames, Wim Crouwel, Paul Rand, Eliott Noyes, Adrian Frutiger), modernism generated a consistent array of material and spatial fabrications intent on an intimate relation between the logic of construction and use. Baudrillard's analysis and, in effect, the whole of semiotics during the 1960s, outlined the multiplication of functional discourses, including the dysfunctional and inessential aspects of cultural uses, those use values that were at odds with a universal language. Nonetheless, the huge changes in spatial culture incurred via the realization of glass architecture and repetitive logic gave current architecture its catalog of basic and undeniable systems of building, if not representation. The very material things at which Jacques Tati poked fun in his film *Playtime* (1967) are what survive today as the compelling ingredients in contemporary architecture. The cultural regimentation of modernism has, however, given way to even more supple and open-ended arrangement of functions.

[3] Scarcity of land is directly linked to the concept of location in real estate.

[4] Baudrillard points to Marcel Mauss's theory of the gift to explain the differentiated, singular, irreplaceable aspect of symbolic exchange.

[5] Danish semiotician Louis Hjelmslev (1899–1965) developed the concept of *glossematics*, which consists of both linguistic and nonlinguistic languages. He also conceived of a system known as *connotative* semiotics, later taken up by Roland Barthes in *The Fashion System*. Hjelmslev referred to the elements of this connotative system as units of *style* that exist on an expression plane different than a content plane.

[6] Winfried Nöth, *Handbook of Semiotics* (Bloomington: Indiana University Press, 1990), 437.

[7] Pleasure is used here to describe the moment when a building works *on all levels* with work being a reference to both use-logic and beauty.

Aluminum

A metallic chemical element, symbol Al, atomic number 13, atomic weight 26.98154. It is silver(y), a code color for lightweight performance metals.

Glass

A material made from hot liquid materials that, when cooled, do not crystallize but rather remain in an amorphous state. It is so viscous that it becomes solid, yet is completely transparent. "Above all, though, glass is the most effective conceivable material expression of the fundamental ambiguity of atmosphere: the fact that it is at once proximity and distance, intimacy and the refusal of intimacy, communication and noncommunication. Whether as packaging, window, or partition, glass is the basis of a transparency without transition; we see, but cannot touch. The message is universal and abstract."[2]

Sea-foam Green

Pantone 3375; 34% Cyan, 0% Magenta, 24% Yellow, 0% Black
Where does the interest for this color come from?

A

At the seaside, sea-foam green finds the origin of its name: a particular color used to mildly contrast with the sky and that connotes aquatic or marine functions. It is the color of light refracted through water or glass.[3]

B

In postwar American public schools, dormitories, community centers, etc., institutional green was a color used as a neutralizing agent in interiors, much the way architects now use white paint. Studies in spatial psychology revealed that this color proved to be pleasant, a calming effect in the peripheral vision, and not at all distracting.

A+B

Sea-foam green is simultaneously nature and artifice, a color that is clearly not of the earth but of the liquid or ambient conditions of water and sky.

[1] Separated by films of liquid, foam is a material consisting of microgas bubbles. Although thermodynamically stable, a foam is mechanically fragile. *Concise Encyclopedia of Science and Technology* (New York: McGraw-Hill, 1997), 816.

[2] Jean Baudrillard. *The System of Objects* (New York: Verso, 1996), 41–42.

[3] Cf. "Beach View Dealey Plaza," 59.

xy=z

There is something about an escalator. Its interior is made up of a series of mechanical and electrical systems that revolve endlessly about themselves, yet as it moves and does not go anywhere, the people on it do not move yet they are transported diagonally through space. Unlike an airplane or an automobile, those vehicles that move through space, the escalator is a "vehicle" that is part of the infrastructure of building, fixed in place with the stair on the everpresent move. While the escalator goes nowhere, we exploit, just like Heidegger's bridge over the Rhine,[1] the machine that takes us in the z direction by extrapolating the x and the y. As we move through space, we are upwardly mobile on the escalator, yet it is a casual movement, languid, temporal. Where elevators pulverize time by cutting through floor slabs at the rate of 1.5 per second, escalators need voids or slots in the floors to move through, slowly, *slo-mo*—and what about its silence? Or the mysterious, glaucous light[2] briefly but rhythmically flashing from its interior? Isn't that sea-foam green?

Except for New York, North American cities are escalator cities, not elevator cities. Mostly horizontal, slightly vertical. But even New York uses them to extend the ground up into the interior of tall buildings, department stores, museums, etcetera—framing atriums, connecting to subways, diagonally relentless.

[1] See Martin Heidegger, "The Question Concerning Technology," in *Basic Writings* (New York: Harper and Row, 1982).

[2] Cf. "The Glaucous Paradise," 48.

Binaries, Monologics, and Multiplicities

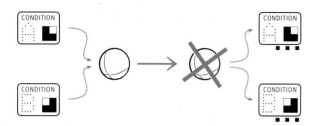

1
Conditions A + B » attempted synthesis » synthesis rejected » A and B persist

3
Conditions A + B » attempted synthesis » B rejected » A persists

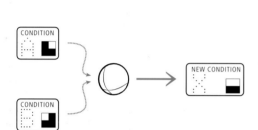

2
Conditions A + B » attempted synthesis » synthesis successful » Condition X

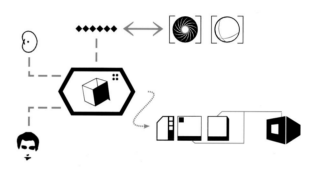

4
Multiplicities

A: Binary
Figures 1 and 2
Binary thinking has long dominated Western discourses. From Cartesian dualist logic to the symbolic formal language of the computer, thinking in terms of contrasts and opposition is fundamental to our thought patterns. Indeed, conventional regimes of signs, languages, and codes are often located by the persistent and, indeed, natural contextualization of one thing and its opposite within a single field. I think this point is revealed in Roland Barthes's statement "that beauty may only be judged by comparison." The questions are: Aren't we beyond this mode of thinking? Haven't we become bored by the equilibrium of the binary? Didn't we learn that nonequilibrium is the source of order?

B: Monologic
Figure 3
It is often the concern for progress in thinking itself that propels the development of a postlinear or postbinary logic, for somehow it seems that the ballast of such logics prevent us from lifting off into a zone beyond the comparative, out of the gravity of the antagonistic world of opposing forces. Wouldn't a world of singularities be a pure one, where any one thing, any one process, would never be countered by its presumed opposite?

C: Multiplicities
Figure 4
The undecidable world does not produce paralysis but rather more and more possibilities—a radical piling up of ways to move and think, sets of freedoms once unthinkable, now viable. These are permeable landscapes, always moving, never stopping to be compared as in the binary world. But how to avoid the danger of uncritical thinking where *more and more* may not result in a compelling process of incorporation?[1]

(A + B) x C = The Gyroscopic Logic
The binary can never be destroyed, only momentarily abandoned. The monological can never be achieved, only momentarily simulated. The multiple can alleviate futility, but only if you control the possibilities.

[1] "Ideas are multiplicities; every idea is a multiplicity or a variety. In this Riemannian usage of the word *multiplicity* (taken up by Husserl, and again by Bergson), the utmost importance must be attached to the substantive form; multiplicity must not designate a combination of the many and the one, but rather an organisation belonging to the many as such, which has no need whatsoever of unity in order to form a system." Gilles Deleuze, *Difference and Repetition*, trans. Paul Patton (New York: Columbia University Press, 1994), 182.

Diptych[1]: Lever House[2]

Vague repetition: self-similar halves

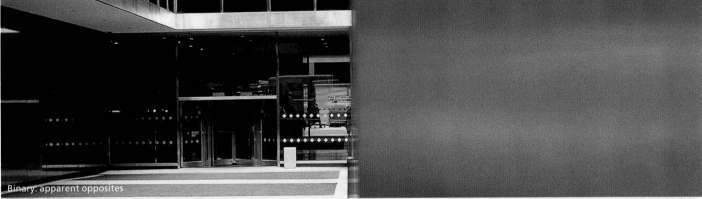

Binary: apparent opposites

Bi-univocal: in-between pairing

The line that describes the center of the diptych is always variable. It is always spatial and it indicates a field of play.[3] The line is formed by the edges of two images, two forms, or as a line that splits the singular image or space into two.

Axiom: The diptych is always the beginning of the many, even when it resembles the One or the Binary.

[1] The word *diptych* comes from a combination of the Roman *dis,* "twice," and *plusso,* "to fold," meaning thus "folded into."

[2] Headquarters for Lever Brothers, Inc., makers of excellent soap products. Designed by Gordon Bunshaft of Skidmore, Owings, and Merrill. New York City, corner of Park Avenue and 54th Street. Completed 1952. The building consists of a two-story horizontal courtyard building lifted up on square stainless-covered columns. Above the mat building is a twenty-one-story, forty-foot-wide curtain wall office tower.

[3] Imagine a film where between each cut a period of a few seconds of blackness existed, forcing cinema to make the splice a longer moment; the cut would become a time-full condition.

Difference and Repetition

Example I

The Platonists used to say that the not-One distinguished itself from the One, but not the converse, since the One does not flee that which flees it.[1]

Scenario A

One = repetition, i.e., one of many/Not-One = difference, i.e., unlike any other of the Ones. One moves on a path toward a horizon. Not-One sees the path of One and moves to the opposite path. Here, difference has no identity other than to say that it has nothing to do with One. Not-One generates difference by fearfully moving away from One.

Scenario B

Not-One = repetition/One = difference. Not-One moves on a path as a nonentity, with no thought, toward *any* horizon. One moves past Not-One on the same path. Difference as a positive. Desire as a movement, a flow. One generates difference by seeing a horizon.

Example II

Think of the phrase *make a difference*. What is the motivation to state this? Identity? Hubris? Altruism? Desire?

Example III

For there is no other aesthetic problem than that of the insertion of art into everyday life. The more our daily life appears standardized, stereotyped, and subject to an accelerated reproduction of objects of consumption, the more art must be injected into it in order to extract from it that little difference which plays simultaneously between other levels of repetition, and even in order to make the two extremes resonate—namely, the habitual series of consumption and the instinctual series of destruction and death.[2]

— Repetition should not be relegated to the status of ground just because "life" repeats itself.
— Standardization should not be confused with ritual, with life's incessant reiterations.
— The appearance of difference within replication is like freshly fallen snow — each flake is different, yet all we see is white.
— Difference may be injected like a homeopathic drug — not as antibiotic but as organic sameness.

Example IV

— Deleuze might ask if the knot in a piece of plywood is fundamentally different from the surrounding grains or if it is merely a strange enlargement within a fully repetitious field.
— He also demands that difference not be so alienating, so evil.[3]

Example V

Repetition as innovation, as mechanism of liberation, of life and death; repetition as will, as the opposite of the laws of nature; repetition as new morality beyond habit and memory; repetition that only attains tension and creativity with the fissures of difference, with disequilibrium, innovation.[4]

Example VI

Among the more vernacular definitions of the word *grain* is this one: "the essential character or logic of a thing." The questions of the fluid and, indeed, of difference and repetition will be found in the grain. In the concept and material concerns of the grain lie real structural systems consisting of repetitive lines, units, or cells making essentially infinite patterns — Zip-a-tone screens, honeycomb cell structures, corrugations of all kinds, enlarged photography, wood (veneers), refracted light in swimming pools, raked-gravel Zen gardens, etc.

[1] Gilles Deleuze, *Difference and Repetition*, trans. Paul Patton (New York: Columbia University Press, 1994), 28.

[2] Ibid., 293.

[3] Ibid., 29. "Difference must leave its cave and cease to be a Monster."

[4] Ignasi de Solà-Morales, *Differences*, trans. Graham Thompson, ed. Sarah Whiting (Cambridge, MA: MIT Press, 1996), 38.

The Multiple Unconscious

Position A: Freud's Theory of the Unconscious
Pretext—dreams, sexuality, deliriousness, hidden territories of desire and actions.

Position B: Jean Baudrillard's Theory of the Technological Unconscious
In his introduction to *The System of Objects*, Jean Baudrillard outlines both the concept of the system and the zone where a discourse on objects may begin. Rather than restate the functional mandate of an object system, the book concerns itself with the ways in which people relate to the field of structured systems of objects, including the aspects of behavior and cultural connotation, leaving behind the ballasted logic of premanufactured purposes and responses. Within this interactive assessment of human relations in the object-filled landscape lies a plane distinct from this spoken system, a more strictly structured plane, a structural plane transcending even the functional account of objects. This is the technological one. The technological plane is an abstraction; in ordinary life we are practically unconscious of the technological reality of objects. Yet this abstraction is profoundly real; it is what governs all radical transformations of our environment.[1] By first assigning an abstract value to a metadiscourse on technology, then stating its real condition in the world, Baudrillard at once raises the idea of the essential[2] nature of objects within a technological realm. It is as though our world is organized around a conceptual and thoroughly ineffable language of engagement with the technical strata of objects in our environment. In fact, it is the endless totality of these objects that constitutes our environment, a field where cell phones, buildings, and trees are spatial and machinic interfaces with varying degrees of proximity to the body. If the vast matrix of objects (both natural and man-made) is our environment, does this mean that the technological aspect of our unconsciousness is ground zero in our understanding of the events, actions, and, indeed, the transformations of our world?

Position C: Fredric Jameson's Theory of the Political Unconscious
Jameson's rethinking of economics as a ground against which all other cultural production may be measured comes out of Marxist rhetoric. Marx's economies of fabrication and extraction as transformed by an information economy of immaterial means of producing data is not, for Jameson, a complete model of describing the world system. While he does not entirely need to jettison a Marxist-based superstructure economic analysis to reach a new reading of production, the interconnection of the cultural text to the market catapults Jameson's arguments past the modernist polemics of corporate homogeneity into a differentiated, if still unconscious, contemporary world. Where the texts of the economic and the cultural meet, the political unconscious is to be found, as we are all implicated in myriad social relations in any given political economy.[3]

Position D: Felix Guattari's Theory of the Schizo-Unconscious
The production of subjectivity is possible when an individual or a group is able (free) to generate an idea, position, or, indeed, a feeling about the state of affairs of his, her, or their environment. Whether the subject is singular or collective, subjectivity is understood to be the bundled pathways of experience that intimately localize us. Guattari argues for a collapse of psychological and social machines into the material, technological machines of information in order to densify the subjective discourse, creating an extended version of what he calls *collective equipment*, the apparatus that combines the abstract with the machinic. With such deeply saturated structures in our environment, like those of mass media, cinema, and computerization in general, it isn't possible to keep this phenomenon unhinged from the social demands of life in the city. In the search for a completely heterogeneous field, Guattari crosses the nonhuman machines of subjectivication (noninterpersonal structures) with the "faculties of the soul" in a nonbinary production of subjectivity. Beyond a superpositioning of machines and families (of people, of languages, of aesthetics), Guattari suggests nothing less than a new mixture of unconscious strata of the subjective discourse.[4]

New Formula of the Unconscious:

$$\frac{(B+D)C}{A} = \text{the Gyroscopic Unconscious}$$

[1] Jean Baudrillard, *The System of Objects* (New York: Verso, 1996), 4–5.

[2] Heidegger's concept of the essence of technology, as outlined in his famous text *The Question Concerning Technology,* is another position to be referenced here. Baudrillard's position is, however, at odds with Heidegger's idea that modern technology is a system of overdetermined machines. Whereas Heidegger's essentialist and abstract discourse on technology rejects the mental relations possible in an actional mode, Baudrillard's abstracted plane of unconsciousness is integral to a full understanding of an object.It seems that the essential, that abstract mode of being, is not defined by use, function, or aesthetics. The condition of essence, in fact, wards off every attempt to concretize it.

[3] See Fredric Jameson, *The Geopolitical Aesthetic* (Bloomington: Indiana University Press, 1992).

[4] Felix Guattari, *Chaosmosis* (Bloomington: Indiana University Press, 1992). Guattari writes that after he rejected a Freudian dualist discourse, he adopted "an unconscious of Flux and of abstract machines rather than an Unconscious of structure and language. I don't, however, consider my 'schizoanalytic cartographies' to be scientific theories. Just as an artist borrows from his precursors and contemporaries the traits which suit him, I invite those who read me to take or reject my concepts freely. The important thing is not the final result but the fact that the multicomponential cartographic method can co-exist with the process of subjectivication." See Chapter 1, "The Production of Subjectivity," 12–13.

Logo[1]

Expanding Corporate Systems

The corporate logo is a powerful symbol in our world, not only of the company itself but also of the idea that, like a Chinese character, it is a signform for a larger narrative.[2] In the contemporary world, the image of the corporation is a Rorschach-like figure, capable of conjuring responses that probe the depths of our cultural subconscious. While the immediacy of recognition is the success of any logotype, it is as a vortex through which the particular company's history is written that a logo extends itself into our imagination. Whatever the company does, whether it dominates a particular market, spills oil on undisturbed shorelines, or makes massive charitable contributions, its identity is thoroughly saturated with these events.

Operating as a Rosetta stone of the NASDAQ landscape, the logo is a singular two-dimensional corpus, a palimpsest of information: TV ads, annual reports, images of the CEO, and controversial headlines, all hypertextualized in our heads. Far beyond being simply the center of a brand identity, the logo is a figure of resistance. Identities of the subject fluctuate; the connotations of the logo remain fixed.

It could be said that the logo is a diagram or sign for the global, corporate, and transnational hegemony that has caused the presumed demise of the polyvocal world. Insofar as the logo is an icon that is not translatable (as it is its own single-character language), it appears everywhere to force its univocity on the world. In the subway system of Singapore, in the streets of São Paulo, in the suburbs of Seattle, on the TV sets of the world, and perhaps even in the wilds of Africa or the Nubian Desert, the logo is purposely unchanging so that its repetitive appearance will imprint itself in our own logography. As a sign system, a corporate logo attempts to be in places where there is an existing or potential market for a company's products; these markets are increasingly the entire world. No place, no means of communicating is immune to the logo. The company wants to expand its market.[3]

Delimiting Territory

In contrast to the deeply saturated effects of the corporate logo, the image of Los Angeles gang identity defines and articulates the specific territory it wishes to

protect. Like small city-states, the quadrants of real ground operated by the gang have virtual walls erected through sheer hubris, if not fratricide. The gang does not want to expand; it wants to cordon off its own groundspace. There is no market-place here, only a brotherhood. But the identifying symbols that the gang employs to delimit territory, such as colors, fashion, cars, and haircuts, give way to the same graphical system that the corporation uses: the logo. Here, the voice of the logo is physical, crafted, singular—one of, and in direct relation to, the corporeal concerns of the group. Only the real limits, the real members are identified through the object-logo—nothing more. Held out to the world from a passing car, it is the first line of media systems employed in the gang's local identification program.

The reliance on the graphic is endemic to all groups. The only difference is the level of repetition.

[1] *Logos*, from the Greek, means discourse.

[2] Chinese (and Japanese) characters are complex forms that are pictographic in nature. Images, objects, and micronarratives are transformed through the arrangement of strokes in each character. In Japan, however, two other written alphabets, katakana and hiragana, have been developed to stand in for many of the Chinese characters (kanji), which most people do not use or have forgotten.

[3] Even though, most often, the corporate structure (as represented by the logo) does not want to dominate land per se in favor of the virtual landscapes of the market (a space theoretically more vast than real ground), the globalized, West-ernized, and suburbanized aspects of mass production seem to eclipse the promise of cost reduction, competition, and accessibility on which laissez-faire capitalism was built.

I flew into Roissy on Pan Am for the first time on 26 August 1982, a week before my twenty-fifth birthday. It was my first trip to Europe.

The plan had been set. I was to work at Aerospatiale in La Courneuve, an industrial suburb north of Paris.[2] I was to live in a dormitory room in the Dutch Pavilion on Boulevard Jourdan at the Cité Universitaire located on the southern edge of Paris, not far from the Peripherique.

Excited about all that lay ahead in Paris, I could not have imagined what kind of a world I was really to step into next.

The walk from the plane to the terminal below ground was mind-blowing. Memory burn. The tunnel was a kind of carpeted brutalism that I had not experienced before—at least it was not like any Rudolph building I had seen.[3] It was light and heavy all at the same time, supersmooth plaster and concrete. It seemed to float like the interior of a submarine, opaque yet buoyant, with relentless indirect

artificial lighting systems directing the disembarking passengers. The tunnel had a camber to it, so there seemed to be a horizon line in the middle, with people in the distance rising and falling in relation to it. Something strangely aquatic about it.

Upon seeing the inaccessible void at the center of the huge concrete torus terminal, I felt as though this place was beyond architecture itself. I suddenly experienced it as a galaxy with its own gravity, its own event horizon and black hole, moving people in the circulation tubes as if they were helpless particles being spun into another time cusp by the effluvial forces acting in the void.

During the autumn, the sun does not set in Paris until 9 P.M. Quite often, after work, I took the RER, the express regional metro system, north to Roissy, to wander around Terminal 1. It was just twenty minutes away from La Courneuve.

There is no more lucid and poetic example of the binary of fixity versus flow than the Charles de Gaulle Terminal 1. A concrete torus is fixed in time, inert and

platonic. Its continuous section extrudes about itself in a circle — indeed, a two-dimensional gyroscope of eternal equilibrium. In its center, aluminum and glass circulation tubes crisscross from low to high, moving passengers through a prophylactic space where the pleasure of being inside is only temporary and always protected. The fixity of the terminal block is analogous to the sedentary and strictly identified subject. The lines moving through it are the plenums and pathways of energies, trajectories, and lines of flight that create new identities. Somehow, though, these lines are accelerated by the terminal; they belong there.

[1] Paul Andreu, chief architect and engineer, Aeroports de Paris. Design 1968. Construction 1970.

[2] The headquarters of the company and the rotor blade factory were located next to one another in this chaotic and extremely rough area. It seemed to be an unclassifiable landscape — somewhat Bronx-like, but not. Neither dense nor vacuous, it was a strange mixture of monstrously long housing slabs (and their attendant voids) and shards of turn-of-the-century building patterns.

[3] Paul Rudolph, American architect (1918–1997). Developed from the 1960s on a formal and material proposition that combined corduroy concrete with the spatial strategies of de Stijl. His best-known example is the Yale University Art and Architecture building.

Four Ambivalent Spaces

Videodrome/Airbag

In David Cronenberg's film *Videodrome*, James Woods witnesses his own transformation from voyeur to participant as he enters into the mirage of televisual space. At first transfixed by the sadomasochistic world of Deborah Harry, Woods steps into the window of projected light that illuminates his dark world. The still photograph captures a moment when the glass surface of the picture tube suddenly gives way to a rubberized soft surface. Two hands holding a gun explode from behind this surface, instantaneously forming a three-dimensional membrane imprinted with the pointed gun. This suddenly animated television screen represents media space as a soft zone of interactivity.

The airbag, meanwhile, projects itself from the opposite space. At the moment of impact between the car and another object, the airbag is instantaneously deployed, exploding from the steering wheel into the face and torso of the driver. At this most tragic instant, the most pliant surface in the vehicle, fully opposed to the steel frame, skin, and glass that is folding under extreme force, becomes the strongest, most resilient, and supportive surface, protecting the body from its otherwise inertial path. For a moment, the body makes its own imprint into the softness of technology. These surfaces of impressionable spatio-temporal forms somehow explain our relation to technology as one both fragile and violent. Further, our relation to technology in bodily terms is often mediated by artificial skins and layers that are specifically designed to at once remove the body from actual contact with the operational aspects of technology and, at the same time, place it closer to the received effects of the machineries below the surface.

Bucket Seat/Jellyfish

The cutaway view of the Mercedes-Benz seat demonstrates the way in which, in ergonomic terms, the supple surface of comfort is really the membrane of removal from the otherwise uncomfortable wireframe structure below. Sheepskin, leather, Naugahyde, crushed velour, vinyls, etc.—these are materials of covering up. The Swatch, meanwhile, is all about uncovering.

Introduced in 1985, the Swatch Jellyfish quickly became one of the most ubiquitous consumer objects of the decade. (How many architects bought this one?) Why? Perhaps because it intruded, however benignly, into the consciousness of fear and ignorance of the operations of technology that is common to us all. Wasn't it also one of the most simply beautiful objects to be mass-produced in some time? Our fascination with technology, often due to its complexity, geometry, materiality, and elegance, is expressed in this watch merely by removing the traditional opaque face that usually covers the mechanism below. At a certain level, legibility is compromised by this design. But this loss incurs another kind of gain. Without a contrasting background, the wearer sees through to technology as object while receiving the effect—that is, knowing the time. Even the translucent band produces an effect on our skin, making a blur of flesh, as if the watch is somehow a part of our natural body.

Roller Coaster/Hillscape

Like the subject-object ambivalence, the concept of figure/ground has also been challenged by the effective demise of the ground as a readable backdrop. The roller coaster at Six Flags Magic Mountain, Valencia, California, is a three-dimensional artificial landscape supported by a massive superstructure designed to simulate the effects of a smooth space somewhere between land and flight. This is the desire to build up, to construct an environment that for no other reason than our pleasure should cover the ground. There is no lament here, however, as if pleasure were such a marginal program to satisfy—only the question of primary concern: Why build up when nature already provides the forms necessary for the satisfaction of pleasure?

The hillscape pictured here is just 300 meters from the roller coaster. This terrain closely approximates the fluid geometry of the track as the natural tectonics loop and bend with the same trajectories. How is it possible to avoid the buildup? By using the naturally deployed landscape? To have laid the track onto the ground may have entered into a complicit arrangement with nature, but domination of territory occurs just the same. Perhaps our skill at imitating nature has been raised to a level where found conditions may not provide an option for technological compromise. But there is always the desire to do nothing where there is already the buildup.

Flower/Root

Nature persists in being used as a phenomenon that humans attempt to control through technology. We also look to nature as a paradigm of beauty, where the processes of development and morphological distortions occur through elegant biological means. The flower is surely an axiom of beauty. Is there anyone who does not find the color, forms, smell, and texture of a flower to be beautiful? Even when it is severed from its connection to the ground and placed in an elegant glass vase (violently domesticated?), it retains its beauty because we concentrate so intently on the flower and not the stem. In our fixation on beauty, our understanding of the complex array of systems that allow the flower to symbolize beauty is lost.

Would it not be quite odd, then, to invert this natural system and privilege the root as the beautiful end of the flower? Would this be the demise of aesthetics? The root supports the flower's iconography by being as ugly as the colorful object is beautiful. In uncovering the root, its own beauty may become, possibly, a sign of the systems of reality that operate far more viscerally than the traditional axioms of the sublime. But who is not interested in beauty? The desire to overcome beauty attacks our guilt surrounding the superficial and the hollow. The desire to continue a maniacal search for it is nothing more than the inalienable right to express pleasure in a spatial medium.

The Cinematic Model

The image is of first concern here. Maybe a Bazinian fact-image[1] or an image that lies behind the surface — that is, a mental image. Perhaps a text-image. But to even speak of images in the context of cinema means to suspend in time, if not completely annihilate, cinematic form altogether. Does one — an architect, no less — dare enter into a medium such as cinema to extract, to surgically remove images from films, some of which are not even frames but are PR shots masquerading as a moment of real footage? How is this practice of zero movement, the annulment of movement, distinguished as productive rather than incursive?

My work is not interested in narrative, episode, or the more obvious ways in which cinema may be seen (and has been thoroughly explored) to approximate architecture. In fact, an obsession with the image, something shared by millions, moves the investigation from architectural form to cultural form as represented by the logic and diagrammatic force of certain cinematic productions. The violence of slowing down film such that it might mirror the static nature of the viewer is as radical a concept as the twentieth century has seen. While one could point to a range of temporal possibilities in film, from the slo-mo sequences of Kurosawa in *Seven Samurai* or Peckinpah in *The Wild Bunch*[2] to structuralist filmmaking from the 1960s,[3] I have chosen to focus on three filmmakers who have, in different ways, composed the diptychal arrangement of the different within the repetitive.

[1] In *What is Cinema?* Andre Bazin developed the concept of the fact-image in relation to neo-realist film. He argued that reality was naked and inherently a part of the filmic medium as expressed in the work of Rossellini, Visconti, and De Sica, Italian directors working just after 1945.

[2] The final battle scene in *Seven Samurai* (1950) takes place in the rain. The wet, almost unfocused images blur the oppositional forces of samurai vigilantes and terrorist outsiders. Slo-mo inserts arrest the action and sound, creating a cusp in time. *The Wild Bunch* (1969) takes up similar themes and actions and, indeed, *Seven Samurai* is a partial blueprint for Peckinpah. Slo-mo in this epic Western describes the idea of violence raised to a hysterically unbelievable level. While *The Wild Bunch* is considered to be the forerunner of current levels of violence in Hollywood, it is even more ruthless on another level: with six cameras running simultaneously, the main shootout scene generated a field from which literally hundreds of cuts could be made. The normal Hollywood film has six hundred cuts. *The Wild Bunch* has over three thousand.

[3] Michael Snow's *Wavelength*, Ernie Gehr's *Serene Velocity*, Andy Warhol's *Sleep*, and the work of Hollis Frampton use virtually no camera movement. The events that pass before the frame are simply perturbations within a near equilibrium situation or pure repetition.

→

Antonioni

From 1959 to 1962, Michelangelo Antonioni produced three films in succession that marked the center of his mature work. Unconsciously constituting a loose trilogy, *L'avventura*, *La notte*, and *L'eclisse* form a compelling and continuous landscape of ennui among bourgeois Italians looking for distractions or simply avoiding the confrontations of relationships. The overwhelming and, indeed, inescapable sense of anomie[4] structures these films, whether through stilted or inarticulate conversation, deadly silence, or the empty landscape. Antonioni's camera positions and photo-images set up the ambivalence of the characters in an equally disturbing and always beautiful setting,[5] placing the point of view between the world of the film and the viewer. Floating obliquely above Vittoria (Monica Vitti) and Riccardo (Francisco Rabal) in the opening scene of *L'eclisse,* or using the furniture and doorways to produce a diptychal spatial field in the same scene (figure 1), the camera composes the binary as a way to describe the world of unstable and undecidable conditions.

Neither realist or moralist, Antonioni opens up a schema of ambivalent relations through the (photo)graphic aspects of flatness, deep focus, and the horizontal and vertical splicing of space. The reiteration of x and y in his images does not organize the world in a Cartesian or dualist fashion so much as it aligns the production of difference, the mental image of disengagement, or the reading of what is beyond the surface within a common index or physical space. My meditations on Antonioni are therefore motivated by the diagrammatic formal logic of the diptych that organizes visual phenomena into self-similar halves (vague repetition), apparent opposites (binaries), and sometimes a third, in-between pairing (bi-univocal).

A long scene in *L'eclisse* that takes place in a bourse in Rome reveals two of these three binary organizations. The first is a horizontal diptych (figure 2) depicting the chaos of the trading floor, a manic entanglement of convulsive bodies, against the serenity of the striated pattern of the trading board, approximating a capitalist signform of the ultimate fluxual landscape. The lower half of the composition at once reveals a frenzy of form that, like a Pollock all-over painting, is simply a repetitive pattern or granular field that is nonetheless organized by the forces at work in the program of the space. Above, a different formal repetition occurs, equally as granular in its own gridded logic. The initial formal difference of the image is actually mediated by a strange equanimity operating at the level of the unit and that Antonioni sets up this image as an unbiased, nonjudgmental field. He cannot decide if the capitalist discourse is one worth bothering with or if the actional, dynamic metropolitan human is the central agent in a progressive and modern world.

The second binary (figure 3) is obliterated by an obstinate third condition when a huge stone column splits the image into an unhinged diptych, a more than obvious voiding of the center line. Antonioni uses the vast blind spot of the column to occlude or dissipate the image and to rid it of spatiality, leaving just the bifurcated bodies of Vittoria and Piero (Alain Delon) as the empty remains of a desperately paralyzed society engaged in the addictive, capitalist world.

[4] The American sociologist Robert K. Merton considered an anomic society to be one with a conflicting sense of futility, lack of purpose, and emptiness and despair. He follows Emil Durkheim's study of anomic suicide, furthering the concept that when an individual's goals and current social position are incompatible with those of a prevailing society, withdrawal ensues.

[5] It is unavoidable here to refer to Rem Koolhaas's concept of the "terrifying beauty of the twentieth century" as a diptych framed by tumult and progress.

→

1

3

2

4

Godard

Jean-Luc Godard's production over the last forty years has relentlessly explored critical cinema and its forms of communicating cultural and political territory. Once stating that "cinema is the truth 24 times a second," Godard later condemned this position with its inverse, "cinema is a lie 24 times a second," no doubt conceding that truth is a discourse of futility unmatched in this century and, at the same time, invoking all that *Rashomon*[6] had to teach us. Such a recanting of position further reveals not just the dismissal of realism in cinema but also that there is something inherently binary at the core of thinking, as if no single image could be both a *fact* image and *just* an image. But Godard has never really been that reductive in his thought. Put simply, Godard has constructed an aphorism that is a model of multiple thinking. Indeed, as Deleuze suggests about Godard's opening up: *Given one image, another image has to be chosen which will induce an interstices between the two. This is not an operation of association, but of differentiation, as mathematicians say, or of disappearance, as physicists say: given one potential, another one has to be chosen, not any whatever, but in such a way that a difference of potential is established between the two, which will be productive of a third or of something new. This is the method of the AND.*[7]

Two film images from Godard reveal the method of the AND through the diptych. They are emblems for a practice of thinking that Godard has revealed in many other ways and films.

The first image is from *Weekend* (1967), a film Godard made as a tragicomic analysis of late capitalist bourgeois life. Summarized in the title as a concept of leisure time as commodity, the film delivers the final blow to a Marxist structure of economies, fetishes, and infantile urges in the consumer landscape. During the central scenes, a massive traffic jam resulting from multiple car crashes in the Parisian near-countryside brings to a halt all sense of progress, of movement, of consuming the landscape with the car. Godard's strange death knell to consumer society is sounded with tremendous ambivalence. A seven-minute tracking shot parallel to the road renders the emotions of impatience and the blasé with equal force, shifting the hysteria of death from the body to the object: the automobile

itself. Roland (Jean Yanne) and Corinne (Mireille Darc), the film's case-study bourgeois couple at odds with one another from the beginning, slowly move forward to their own vehicular and cultural demise.

Figure 4 (a photo still, not a frame from the film) depicts the couple in the middle ground of the local apocalypse taking place around them. Roland, bloodstained[8] but still casually smoking a Gitane, and Corinne move through the white smoke desperate to find the nearest surviving automobile. They occupy roughly the right half of the frame, while to the left, two dead figures lie in deep perspectival relation to one another. As the road curves off into whiteness and all of the automobiles are visually eclipsed by smoke, Roland and Corinne occupy a strange, flattened field, their bodies disengaged from perspectival space because there is no depth of field between them—they are in the same plane. Their upright bodies reiterate the vertical axis. The lifeless bodies on the left, conversely, redescribe depth via perspective, the limits of experience through death, and the horizontal axis. Within a theoretically and optically singular field, Godard overlays two different spatial and political conditions.

Nouvelle Vague (1990) is the film from which the second image is taken. Split in two, the film is about a man who returns to a place, a large estate, that he has not come from. The man has two different names, Roger Lennox and Richard Lennox (Alain Delon), one for each half of the film. *Nouvelle Vague* is both diptychal and symmetrical, as Richard Lennox appears after Roger has drowned in a lake on the estate and claims to be his brother. First, it is the same man (Delon playing both parts) who is returning. He claims to be fraternally related but is in fact the other. Second, there is the possibility that it is Roger who has returned to life and it is he who will inhabit the second half of the film.

Godard amplifies this use of vague repetition when he inverts, during the credit sequence, the film's name into *Vague Nouvelle*.[9] Further, the final dialog repeats in aphoristic style phrases such as "Where there's making, there's faking," and "Not the same, another." But it is in figure 5 that we see Godard use the apparent opposite strategy to formalize the condition of the AND.

5

Roger Lennox enters the film via a roadside incident. Coming from nowhere, going nowhere, he is run off the road by an oncoming truck. Godard positions the camera such that a large tree occludes one half of the scopic field from which Lennox seems to be futilely attempting to escape. The running figure and two autos are elements in a classical perspectival space of fore-, middle, and background with a sky of whiteness that severs this scene from any other referential system. On the left half of the frame, the tree is juxtaposed as a nonlinear field. There is no depth, no reference to the things that Lennox is running from, only reference to a world of nature that he may be running to. The tree is only an idea of nature in this frame, a pictogram of the swirls and eddies that make up the flows of univocal discourses. Each piece of bark is like a pixel or an aleph, no more important than the next — a punctum, as Paul Virilio would say.

Godard's diptych could be conveniently analyzed, in the final account, as pure binary — machines, speed, and force versus the inexorable flows of nature — or the tree representing the death of real space via the electronic paradigm versus the palpable anxiety of deeply lived space. For Godard, however, it is both and many more. Deleuze states, "Godard is not a dialectician. What counts with him is not two or three, or however many you like, it's AND, the conjunction AND." [10]

[6] A 1950 film by Akira Kurosawa that tells the story of a murder from the points of view of four characters. All four accounts differ, describing the nonlinear conditions of history or that every event's recording is prone to revision.

[7] Gilles Deleuze, *Cinema 2: The Time-Image*, trans. Hugh Tomlinson and Robert Galeta (Minneapolis: University of Minnesota Press, 1989), 179–180. Deleuze developed the concept of the AND as an overcoming of the verb *to be*. As philosophy is always in search of attributive judgment of what is, it never allows for a multiplicity, for a buildup of conjunction or what Deleuze calls a "stammering" of language. See also Gilles Deleuze and Felix Guattari, *A Thousand Plateaus*, trans. Brian Massumi (Minneapolis: University of Minnesota Press, 1987), and, for a brilliant conversational analysis of Godard's work, Kaja Silverman and Harun Farocki, *Speaking about Godard* (New York: New York University Press, 1998).

[8] Godard abstracted the violence of the film into the coda of coloration and hysteria by saying, "It's not blood, it's red."

[9] One is reminded here of the title of Marcel Duchamp's film, *Anemic Cinema* (1927). *Anemic* is an anagram of *cinema*.

[10] Gilles Deleuze, "Interview: Three Questions about 'Six Fois Deux,'" *Son + Image* (New York: Museum of Modern Art, 1992), 40.

→

6

7

Ozu

To precede Yasjiro Ozu with two European directors working within the context of the history of art and, indeed, of the Western system of meaning-making assemblages is to dramatize his relation to the production of symbolic meaning. Ozu is the most Japanese of all directors precisely because he operates within a monological field of virtually pure repetition. Indeed, his films' subject matter, styles, formal construction, stories, and actors all seem to repeat themselves unapologetically across more than three decades of filmmaking. His *oeuvre* is an all-encompassing horizon, a field. But embedded deep within Ozu's work is a binary theme that can be found even in Antonioni: the dilemma of the empty and the full.

Deleuze writes: *Between an empty space or landscape and a still life properly so-called there are certainly many similarities, shared functions and imperceptible transitions. But it is not the same thing; a still life cannot be confused with a landscape. An empty space owes its importance above all to the absence of a possible content, whilst the still life is defined by the presence and composition of objects which are wrapped up in themselves or become their own container.*[11]

Ozu's best-known work, *Tokyo Story*, has often been called a masterpiece, a somewhat strange label, given the repetitious nature of the work. Nonetheless, it is a classic example of his obsession with the anomic relations between generations in the extended family. Made in 1953, while the machineries of postwar Westernization had just begun to turn, *Tokyo Story* constructs the familiar narrative of the dissolution of the love and respect children should have for their parents. Here, an elderly couple visit their children in Tokyo from provincial Japan, only to find that the son and the daughter are too immersed in their own lives to care for them. In a beautiful scene (figure 6), the parents are seated on the sea wall at Atami, to which their children have sent them off for an erstwhile alternative vacation. Ozu uses discontinuity at this moment as a purely formal compositional strategy that creates a minor form of difference with repetition. With no action to precipitate it, in the next shot, the man and the woman have changed places, she now on the left and he on the right. Figure 7 further illustrates this minor form of difference — not through editing, but through cultural nuance. The couple's daughter and daughter-in-law sit side by side in the traditionally nonconfrontational Japanese structure. Wearing kimonos that are exactly the same, the two women seem to differ only in the way in which their hands are folded.

One is compelled to say nothing more about Ozu.

[11] Deleuze, *Cinema 2*, 16.

Contours

The buildings in this book do not have excessive theoretical value placed on their forms and geometries.
There is no assumption that an architectural position
that incorporates multiple methods of thinking,
employs different tectonic strategies where necessary,
and believes that both the use-value and symbolic value
of programs determine form would be so reductive
as to compact an entire set of possibilities into one
formal logic. Instead, the work attempts to pry open
a logical space between the ends of scenario-based
architecture and geometry-as-content architecture.
Yet the search for a plane of consistency is also at work
in the practice, not simply an endeavor of diversity or
comprehensiveness.

From terrain and surface mapping to repetitive structural logics, contours are the physical surfaces and systems
that govern both the data and the intuition of the
work. They are the manifold conditions of the physical,
static, and cultural forces at play.

Euclidean

Different Kinds

All architectural construction is made up of Euclidean geometry. This is inescapable because the lines of light and gravity are (most) parallel within the world that we experience every day. Only astronomically are these forces understood to converge, hyperbolically, in the infinity of space, crossing and recrossing. This fact, such an overwhelming physical and scopic limit, along with the upright body, has dominated not only the production of all architectural space (that which is lived and experienced) but also the pragmatic theories surrounding tectonic logic and programmatic directness.

Euclidean geometry has been understood as a *kind* of geometry, distinct from topological or Riemannian geometry, for instance, as if today we have a choice of geometries in our move to represent one or more realities in building.[1] As stated, we do not have a choice. But *culturally*, we do have a choice beyond the forces at work in the physical world of our terrestrial life. In fact, it is clear that many architects adhere strictly to the gravitational and Cartesian aspects of Euclidean geometry in the search for forthrightness and possibly for timelessness *and* as a public form of resistance to the kinds of complex geometries that are argued for in contemporary architectural debate. In fact, many architects unconsciously use these arguments as cultural and architectural axioms, as the same sort of definitive proofs on which Euclidean geometry was postulated. Just as Euclidean geometry has its limits, however, these arguments attempt to forge a morality that is equally limited.

The modern history of physics and mathematics tells us that the postulates of Euclidean geometry, however, do not hold up at certain scales, so it must be concluded that there are, in fact, different kinds of geometry, ones that operate locally or gigantically. I suggest a different way to read Euclidean geometry, such that it might be seen as part of a larger supergeometrical system.

Curvature: Degree Zero

Riemann introduced the auxiliary concept of *curvature of space*, which is a much more complicated mathematical structure. Euclidean space, then, has a curvature of degree zero in analogy to the plane, which is a surface of zero curvature. Euclidean space occupies the middle ground between the spaces of positive and negative curvature.[2] It is here posited that *all* geometry is a description of flexure or of bending, part of a dynamic system of forces that make up the physical world. Although we must resolve these forces in buildings by finding equilibrium among the structural conditions acting on them, they are expressions of a dynamic system nonetheless. If Euclidean geometry operates at degree zero curvature, it is simply one moment in a scale of flexure, one where the resolution of forces produces straightness. Indeed, if a line is straight or curved, it is still part of a system of lines (columns, beams, bents, trusses, cables, rods, etc.) that describes the forces acting on a site, a program, an eye, a psyche.[3] The box, therefore, is not simply a known or conservative deployment of geometry or an expedient way to build. It is an aggressive means to shape forces, no different than any other mode of tectonic resolution, because it is part of one supergeometrical system.[4]

[1] "It will be readily understood that the philosophical insight into the two-fold nature of space became possible only after mathematics had made the step from Euclid's geometry to non-Euclidean geometries. Up to that time physics had assumed the axioms of geometry as the self-evident basis of its description of nature. If several kinds of geometries were regarded as mathematically equivalent, the question arose which of these geometries was applicable to physical reality; there is no necessity to single out Euclidean geometry for this purpose." Hans Reichenbach, *The Philosophy of Space and Time* (New York: Dover Publications, 1958), 6.

[2] Ibid., 10.

[3] Erwin Panofsky, *Perspective as Symbolic Form* (New York: Zone Books, 1991), must be consulted here, particularly Section I, which addresses the distortions of horizontal and vertical lines occurring through the retina. He writes, "The orthogonals of a building, which in normal perspective construction appear straight, would, if they were to correspond to the factual retinal image, have to be drawn as curves. Strictly speaking, even the verticals would have to submit to some bending" (33).

[4] Reichenbach, *Philosophy of Space and Time*, 35. "Geometry is concerned solely with the simplicity of a definition, and therefore the problem of empirical significance does not arise. It is a mistake to say that Euclidean geometry is 'more true' than Einstein's geometry or vice versa, because it leads to simpler metrical relations."

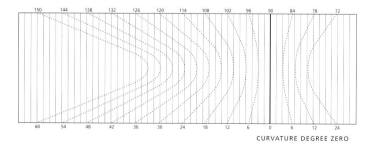

CURVATURE DEGREE ZERO

Osculation—a mathematical term meaning the contact of one curve with another, at a given point, of the highest order possible out of all curves in a family of curves.

Point of osculation—a point on a curve at which two branches have a common tangent and each branch extends in both directions of the tangent. Also called a *tacnode* or a *double cusp*. The origins (centers) of each curve must lie on the same line in order to achieve pure smoothness. At the point of osculation, two arcs of different trajectories, different values (and meanings) align without a kink, fold, or violent irruption. The arcs form a continuous line, a supersmooth and potentially complex line, one built out of the accumulation of centers, a polycentric line.

Along a bending path or a curve is a trajectory of ideas that refuses straightness. This type of line and curving surface attracts us because we realize that the movement of the phenomena of the world are contained in the geometry — pathways of energy relentlessly shaping the abstract programming of our desires. Our control over these curving plenums is operable only to the extent that we are able to arrange them from all the possible and existing pathways. Further, it is argued that all curvature is lying behind[1] the gridded world and that if we choose to recognize the human body or a freeway off-ramp as a signform of the hyperbolic space of non-Euclidean geometry, we engage in the futility of representation; at the same time, we revel in the pleasure of ineptitude, of our own obsessive reiterations of what can never be fully visualized.[2] But why would we explore curvature if we didn't believe that the hyperbolic space of non-Euclidean geometry were somehow operable, not as an autonomous cultural agenda but as a reasonable method to explain conditions as vague as "flow" or as specific as a turning radius?[3]

The projects that follow take up the osculating curvature of smooth geometries because physical space is irreducibly Euclidean and, therefore, the lived experiences and the possible performativity of life in cities and buildings calls forth the need to integrate the supple line into a Cartesian (binary) world. Indeed, the osculatory aspect of life's movements must be seen as multiple arcs and manifold curves in our psychological restructuring of the city.

[1] The deviations in Euclidean geometry are very small and unobservable in everyday life.

[2] "It has occasionally been maintained by mathematicians who have worked a great deal in non-Euclidean geometry that they can gradually visualize it. The proponents of the theory of relativity argue that the visualization of Euclidean geometry is the result of habit, and that we could gradually acquire the ability to visualize non-Euclidean geometry. One must not forget, however, that very little is gained by such a statement, because we do not know yet what is to be understood by 'visualization of non-Euclidean geometry.'" Hans Reichenbach, *The Philosophy of Space and Time* (New York: Dover Publications, 1958), 48.

[3] Note that the point of osculation is a point of *connection*. Radii connect segments. "Connection indicates the way in which decoded and deterritorialized flows boost one another, accelerate their shared escape, and augment or stroke their quanta." Gilles Deleuze and Felix Guattari, *A Thousand Plateaus*, trans. Brian Massumi (Minneapolis: University of Minnesota Press, 1987), 220.

Structure

Two methods of working with structural conditions during the design process can be largely classified as *a priori* or *a posteriori* systems. The first is usually organized by a grid, module, or other predetermined and regulated pattern. The logic is based on programmatic analysis, building materials, and a belief that architecture comes out of "structuring elements." Buckminster Fuller (tensegrity systems) and Le Corbusier (the domino frame) provide examples of how the structure sets up a field or a ground for the final envelope and the internal partitioning of space.[1] The second system is simply manifest as the postengineered resolution of forces of a conceptual structure. Not thought of as an insignificant part of the design process, however, here structure is a delay in the coming to terms with the static and physical forces operating in the physical field. Frank Gehry's work is an example of this mode of *a posteriori* structure.[2] My work incorporates both strategies.

Bending

In material applications of structure, bending has two different effects on a system. One is unwanted. When a structural member is bent, this usually means it cannot resist the loads or forces applied to it; an eccentric load causes a column to deflect or bend, a beam may sag if the span is too long, and so on. Another effect is desirable. Depending on how a member works with another element, bending may generate more strength than straight pieces. Metals such as steel and aluminum respond to bending very well. However, the walls of structural members must be thick enough to tolerate the stretching that occurs along the outer edge of the radius.

Radius

Bending invariably involves making a radius in a member or a sheet of material. The radius transfers forces from one direction to another and allows a smooth, possibly cornerless, spatial continuum. I am interested in working with a geometrical system in which a degree of structural logic is inherent as well as the flexibility for which an a posteriori structural system might allow. As such, my work integrates columnar fields with sheet surfaces that have their own structural logic.

Stiffness

Structure generates stiffness through depth. When repeated like a sine curve, a radius produces a corrugation. Materials like brown cardboard and industrial siding provide common examples of how stiffness is generated. In cardboard, the corrugated paper inside is sandwiched between flat sheets to produce a flat panel. Extruded metal siding allows bending along the grain of the extrusion, but not against it.

Composite

Structural systems like origami and the automobile chassis are based on a pattern of folds or welds applied to a sheet of structural material. They incorporate column, beam, and skin out of a single original material, a kind of structural monologic. Though these examples are on a smaller scale than buildings, they provide a potential logic of construction that could dissipate the binary of frame and skin.

[1] In Fuller, there is a one-to-one relationship between all of the elements, a synergy or a kind of Albertian whole where one missing element causes failure in dependent systems. In Le Corbusier, especially as outlined in the five points, the envelope is, in fact, liberated from the structure.

[2] Frank Gehry's projects in the 1990s have largely resolved structural forces within the wall surfaces of the buildings themselves. The Guggenheim Museum at Bilbao, Spain, for instance, has few exposed columns. Because his work is loosely cellular, the irregular stacking of the elements works to bring the forces to the ground without recourse to independent columnar systems.

All the surfaces of the world converge everywhere and all the time.

Scapes are the substrata of experience.   You are a scape.

Fashion/Models

Fashion

The work in this book is part of a fashion system and is in itself a constituted style. The value of architecture is not found in its origin but in its place in the architecture system.

In fashion, the model, like a building, is not usually repeated in reality.

Models

Models. Mechanized outwardly. Intact, virgin within.
Models. Preserved from any obligation towards the art of drama.[1]

Jean Baudrillard explains that the condition of the modern object, its status, is dominated by a productive and linear logic of appearance: the model/series distinction. Mass production usually involves a process of research, development of prototypes, and modeling of potential solutions prior to the extended production run of the object. In industrial terms, the model is the original idea of the object—then it becomes the originating physical artifact to be serially produced. As the model is installed in a commercial system, through mechanical reiteration it becomes available and accessible for everyone. It ceases to live in an isolated world of autonomy, of invention.[2]

The model/series structure is not endemic to all categories of mass-produced objects and certainly not for objects that remain models. Baudrillard points to clothing and cars as clear examples of the model/series scheme, but the difference between two television sets makes it much harder to apply the scheme, as the quality of the image on the screen, the means by which the function of watching comes into play, is of primary concern, not whether it has a black or a brown shell. The object's function here absorbs the differences of status among the televisions and sets into motion a utilitarian privileging to the choice at hand.[3]

In other types of objects, inessential or marginal differences manifest themselves as choice. Baudrillard writes: *The corollary of the fact that every object reaches by way of a serial choice is the fact that fundamentally no object is offered as a serial object, that every single object claims model status. The most insignificant object must be marked off by some distinguishing feature—a colour, an accessory, a detail of one sort or another....The point is, of course, that all these "specific" differences are themselves picked up and mass-produced in serial form. And this secondary seriality is what constitutes fashion. Ultimately, therefore, every object is a model, yet at the same time there are no more models.*[4]

As we live among serialized objects, from computers to clothing, our urge to personalize becomes dependent on the options available to us in the field of commodities.[5]

Architecture might be the perfect example of the medium where there is *always* and *never* the model. Unlike the series object, architecture is never fully prototyped to scale and it is rarely completely crafted and assembled in an industrial process.[6] But when we speak of models in architecture, the model moves from that of the physical object as an original thing to be copied (industrially) to that of the idea or paradigm for architecture. Not typically classified by programmatic type, architectural models are ideas about the whole field. The suburban house in a subdivision, for instance, is a model for economy and planning that has been in operation for fifty years. The plan of the house is basically repetitive and insensitive to site. Though each house is built by hand, it is always part of a series.

When considering the architect as a maker of a model (a singular building with no intention to be repeated), one witnesses most often the attempts from the beginning to personalize or produce difference in the object, to offer a new project. The building is offered to two end-users: the specific client and the culture of architecture in general. The client consumes the building at the level of the personalized and the architecture culture studies it as a potential paradigm. Though the building is not to be repeated, it is subject to seriality on four levels:

I The architect may choose to consciously use the model as a personal paradigm and repeat it until the energy of the model is exhausted through successive iterations.
II The architect may unconsciously repeat the model.
III An altogether different architect may use either I or II above with the same model.[7]
IV Architecture culture may use ideas or essences but not material forms of the model for critical uses. The concepts may thus be progressively absorbed by the culture—and so remembered by history.

Numbers II and III have the potential for, as Baudrillard states, "style deficit." He writes, "In parallel fashion, when we compare the serial object to the model we find that the serial object's physical attributes, just like the technical ones, are distinctly inferior."[8] We have typically seen with items I and IV a more productive use of the idea that architects and their internal culture consume their own models.

---

[1] Robert Bresson, *Notes on the Cinematographer* (Copenhagen: Green Integer, 1997). Bresson refers to the actors in his films as models because he primarily used untrained people in them.

[2] Jean Baudrillard, *The System of Objects* (New York: Verso, 1996), 137.

[3] Ibid., 139–140.

[4] Ibid., 141–142.

[5] In Japan, the contemporary landscape of objects is consistently classified and updated in a phenomenally large number of magazines locally referred to as *manuals*. Each month, magazines such as *Dime* and *Trendy* organize objects not only in simple encyclopedic fashion but also according to status and cultural perception for that month. Entire magazines are devoted to watches, sneakers, skis, scooters, cell phones, etc. Twenty-something men are often referred to as *manual guys* if they are seen to have staked out their entire lifestyle system through these magazines.The desire to express individual uniqueness is framed, then, by the limits of choice (the magazine) and the extension of particular intention. For example, an audiophile may have a technically advanced stereo system and not use it, or a music lover may have a basic system and listen not for high-end fidelity but for the soul of the music.

[6] Vehicles such as motor homes, trailers, houseboats, and possibly airplanes qualify as mass-produced industrial objects, even though there is a handmade aspect in their production.

[7] After Julia Kristeva, we might say that this version of the model is isomorphic in that it has a different lineage or founding, but the same appearance.

[8] Baudrillard, *System of Objects*, 147. This is in direct contrast to Deleuze's idea of the mediator, one who will produce a newer, better model. See Gilles Deleuze, "Mediators," in *Zone 6: Incorporations* (New York: Zone Books, 1992).

Glaucous — light greenish-blue or bluish-green color
Paradise — a place of extreme beauty or happiness

In the contemporary world, with its high-technology luster and corrosive urban mutations as a kind of ambivalent capitalist varnish, one series of cultural surfaces is progressively more liberating and accessible, while others are perhaps Spenglerian[1] in nature, collapsing under the overcoded weight of sex, violence, and myopia. The hum of hard drives, the flickering LEDs, the blinking eyes of the soulless computer,[2] the cathode grains of televised images, the feedback of overdriven guitars and keyboards[3]—we are awash in the glaucous paradise, desperate to find the electronic shadow[4] that Paul Virilio convinced us was out there. Suffering from tinnitus and insomnia, yet never more productive, we are experiencing more pleasure than shock at the new forms of production technique and lifestyle options escalating all around us.

A New Morality?
For J.G. Ballard, the twentieth century has been the time of the unlimited possibility, when ideas and even dreams can be realized through the application of a culturally directed machine. Ballard's work in the 1970s, particularly his trilogy of nightmare novels, *Crash*, *Concrete Island*, and *High-Rise*, which describe, for instance, the mixing of bodily fluids and engine coolant as a potent concoction in the synthesis of the body-machine dialectic (marriage?), articulates the condition of the negative by activating the repressed desires of the reader. In citing the "death of affect" as the primary loss of the century, Ballard concludes optimistically that "this demise of feeling and emotion has paved the way for all our most real and tender pleasures."[5] Ballard is describing, in essence, the strange pleasure of the dystopian landscape where the interpretation of technology (and its effects) is neither fatalistic nor determined, but in fact residing, ultimately, inside one's own head. As our own pathologies guide us beyond the policed state of the externalized, authoritarian world, the privacy of our thoughts and actions conveys the distortions of a posthumanist world. This may constitute or summarize Ballard's response to the breakdowns in the complete modernist apparatus, inspired by the events and fallout of May 1968 as well as by the economic crisis of the early 1970s. In contrast to the anarchy of the Situationists, for instance, Ballard implodes the anxiety of urban fear and decimation back into the self, collecting the energies of reaction as a force for private strategies.

The cartography of this mutated, internalized landscape is, according to Ballard, more honest, perhaps more coherent, and certainly more exploitative of the unlimited condition of the imagination, pushing toward, as Nietzsche did, a new morality. For all of Ballard's attempts to describe a world removed, sequestered from the everyday scene, he voyeuristically invades with video cameras and telescopic devices, his privileged position of observer (often an autobiographical one) dismantled as a binary condition. "Instead, Ballard details a permanent condition of interface, of sheer contiguity, an invasion of the subject so thorough that his frequent use of the word *dream* no longer describes anything interior."[6]

Inside?
In *The Eiffel Tower*, Roland Barthes explores a similar territorial breakdown of the interior-exterior threshold. The Eiffel Tower, the empty, useless,[7] omnipresent object that can be seen from anywhere in Paris, is explored by the tourist not as a symbol of anything primary but rather as an enormous curiosity, mediated by its own repeatable image (either through postcards or real-time vision). As the visitor transgresses the presumed line between out and in, the object itself begins to disappear, the evaporation of its own iconography, replaced by the memories of a million Camcorders. Barthes describes the tower as having two provisions. He calls the first a "technical order"—"the Tower offers for consumption a certain number of performances, or, if one prefers, of paradoxes, and the visitor then becomes an

engineer by proxy."[8] By inspecting the making of the Tower, the visitor may dwell within the object so as to know it. The distortion of the geometry of the base of the Tower, although quadrilaterally symmetrical, when standing next to it, disorients the observer's reading of the object in the field as a vertical line. "Thus the Tower-as-object furnishes its observer, provided he insinuates himself into it, a whole series of paradoxes, the delectable contradiction of an appearance and of its contrary reality."[9] Technology, here, is a subtext to be read at close range, the apparent prop to the emptiness of the superficial object. Contemporarily, we can refer to advertising billboards and corporate office tower skins to find the repressed expression of structure. Once inside the web of the interior, however, the Ballardian interface takes over as the ergonomics of not only the body but the mind collapse into a matrix of forces outlined by the material and spatial conditions of architecture. In this, Ballard and Barthes present a positive approach to the psychopathologies of perception, a dystopia colored by the possibilities of expression, legibility, and, above all, viscerality.

[1] See Oswald Spengler, *The Decline of the West* (New York: Oxford University Press, 1991).

[2] I am referring to Brian Eno's observation that computers do not have enough Africa in them.

[3] Refer to the music of the Velvet Underground (1960s), Suicide (1970s), Glenn Branca and Rhys Chatham (1980s), and Stereolab (1990s). "This event is like an extended chord, like an intensity at an energetic crux of streams of communication, a subjective apprehension offered by the architect in the joy of producing a polyphonic instant in the heart of the chaotic metropolis." Ignasi de Solà-Morales, *Differences*, trans. Graham Thompson, ed. Sarah Whiting (Cambridge, MA: MIT Press, 1997), 102–103.

[4] A perhaps mythical, if not nonexistent, space of silence and visual monochromy, a space where the world's electronic pulses cannot flow through.

[5] J.G. Ballard, Introduction to his novel *Crash*, reprinted in *Re/Search* (San Francisco), no. 8/9, 96.

[6] Jonathan Crary, "J.G. Ballard and the Promiscuity of Forms," in *Zone 1/2: The City* (New York: Zone Books, 1986), 165.

[7] "This pure—virtually empty—sign is ineluctable, *because it means everything*." Roland Barthes, *The Eiffel Tower* (New York: Hill and Wang, 1979), 4.

[8] Ibid., 15.

[9] Ibid., 15–16.

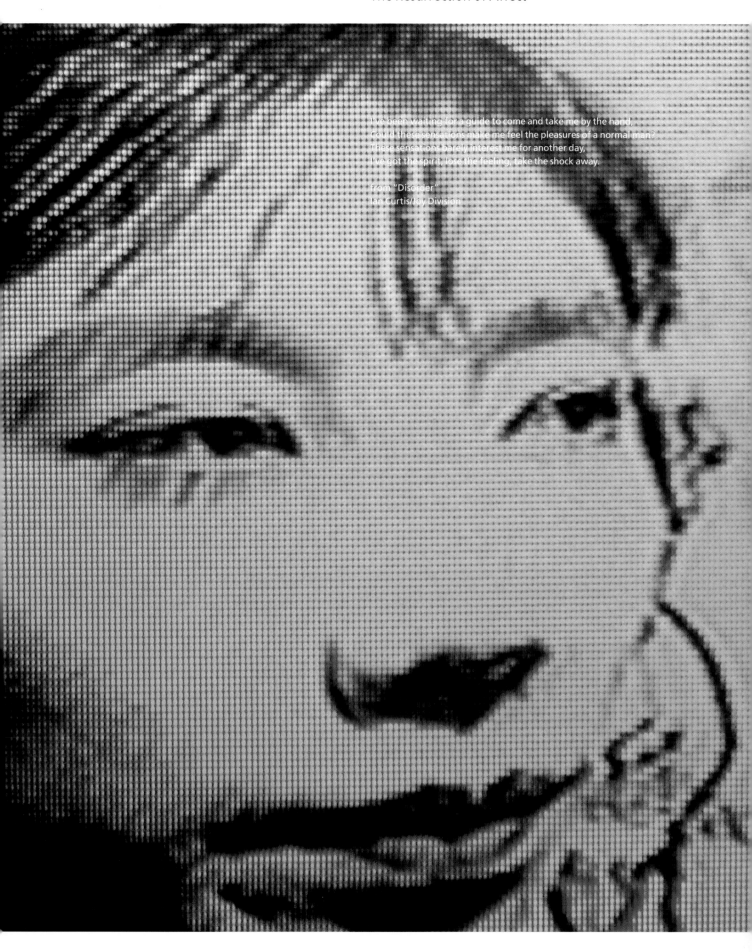

I've been waiting for a guide to come and take me by the hand,
Could these sensations make me feel the pleasures of a normal man?
These sensations barely interest me for another day,
I've got the spirit, lose the feeling, take the shock away.

From "Disorder"
Ian Curtis/Joy Division

Metroplex

In the complex metropolitan environment, the city has no form. The forms of control over time, distance, money, and social space supersede any morphological analysis.

Center and Periphery

Who Won?

The debate on center and periphery concerning the city-structure is over. But who won? The centrists, those wielding high-rises like Zeus and his lightning bolts? Or the peripheralists, those committed to the fate of horizontality? Or still further, are those who refused to participate in this struggle of centralized or diffused power, those who find pleasure in both elevators and blue sky, the winners by default?

Actually, both center and periphery (C&P) won.

Masquerading as opposites, as competitors in a sham debate, C&P devised and choreographed a twentieth-century play of collusion, agreeing that by century's end the truth of the coalition would be disclosed. By now, C&P are not one but many in any metroplex. It is no longer center against periphery but centers *and* peripheries. In terms of both urban morphology and psychogeographics,[1] C&P are forever linked in the construction of physical and mental arrangements of points and arcs.

Loops

Centers are strange conditions. Once the idea of anthropocentric logic, now they are ambivalent. In geometric terms, they exist to locate an origin to an arc or a circle. But, at the same time, we usually believe that the line that emerges in relation to the center is the perimeter that we are searching to construct and the center simply a point whose importance is eclipsed the moment the line is produced. The center is reference but no content, no movement, no energy, no line. In the contemporary North American city, center as tectonic buildup and center as a twenty-four-hour coagulant of people and programs have long been out of registration, two bull's-eyes of similar magnetic polarity, unable to converge.

Chicago and Houston may be compared to explain this phenomenon. The center of Chicago, located at the edge of Lake Michigan, can of course have only radial or peripheral lines across half of the circle (the other half is all water), thereby eliminating from the beginning the possibility of physical centrality. It is a hemicircular city. The Loop downtown is a phantom encircling of a city that will always be bisected. Houston, by contrast, is a city of extreme concentricity. It is surrounded by enough land that its core defines the approximate geometrical center of the city, reinforced by its own loop, the 610 freeway.[2] Chicago, with its decentered core, however, clearly operates as a more traditional city than does Houston's centered downtown.

Arcs

With any center, there must be a periphery. Through terminology like *edge city*, *suburbia*, *exurbia*, *sprawl*, *ring road*, and *conurbation*, the city has been described in the late twentieth century as a binary operation with all peripheral expansions occurring relative to a center. We know that the city is not really the equivalent to the annular redwood, a singular shaft of densely layered circles, and that it is not of the other arborescent model (hierarchical, vertical branching system); it must therefore be polycentric.[3] Unlike the consistent lattice models of the 1960s, however, the real and imagined and extremely inconsistent array of centers and peripheries build up into a field of regions where each new center incrementally reduces the power of all previous centers.[4]

Disks, Halos, and Coronas

Now we know cities are segmented. They have peripheries without centers—anxious lines moving without centralizing sponsorship, acting on their own, becoming ever finer in grain. Across the city, we see other lines that look the same; discovering halos, the aftereffects of the evacuated center.[5]

Let us not confuse cities, however, with the individual. For Deleuze and Guattari, becoming an animal engaged in superhorizontal flows of thought, or for Foucault, practicing "outside thinking" (or thinking "outside the box," the one we put ourselves in) is not the same as an entire city becoming intensely horizontal. Horizontal thought did not make the city; we appropriated it to convince ourselves that the city is as it should be—that the city is always bound to be about difference, even when politics says otherwise. Or that its morphology is like the ultimate book, spreading out all the pages on one level, nothing above or below, all agendas crashing about on a plane of consistency.

[1] A term invented by Guy DeBord to describe the rearticulated city map that one redraws inside one's head. This map is a cognitive surface of points, spaces, terrains, event memories, etc.

[2] A circle with a diameter of 44 miles extending out from the Central Business District can be inscribed on the land before Galveston Bay comes into play. The 610 loop has a diameter of 12 miles.

[3] See Gilles Deleuze and Felix Guattari, "Introduction: Rhizome," *A Thousand Plateaus*, trans. Brian Massumi (Minneapolis: University of Minnesota Press, 1987).

[4] Sanford Kwinter offers a counterargument in his article "La Citta Nuova: Modernity and Continuity," explaining that the new city "is a system then, with no inside or outside, no center and no periphery, merely one virtual circulating substance—force—and its variety of actualized modes—linear, rotating, ascending, combining, transecting." *Zone 1/2: The City* (New York: Zone Books, 1986), 112. His monological approach, giving force its singular space of effect, is an attempt to completely neutralize the binary of center and periphery. As force is *the* substance that fills the plenums of the city, it is only a question as to whether that force atomizes (many microcenters and peripheries) or liquefies (continuing flows).

[5] Deleuze and Guattari, *A Thousand Plateaus*, 208–209.

Terrain Vague/Gone

Empty

GS In the metroplex, one thing seems to always be missing: Where are the people?

DA Inside.

GS Inside? How is it possible, in cities where there is so much openness, so much freedom to move, so much sheer exteriority, that interiors precede and maintain sovereignty over exteriors? I don't get it!

DA Well, there's a lot going on inside[1] and because there is so much space, time and distance are easily distorted.

GS Hmmm. I understand that most of us work inside buildings, live in largely opaque houses and apartments, and even entertain ourselves inside cinema complexes and bars, but beyond that, I suspect what you are saying is that the event of circulating among these places is simply about connection, point to point.

DA That's not it completely. You know *The Production of Space,*[2] right?

GS Some of it. It, like most books of that intensity, gives me a headache after a while!

DA Me too, but there is a part in there about "contradictory space" that really stuck with me. Lefebvre implicates the Cartesian urban space, played out in the grids of streets and rectangular matrices of the tectonic infill and even in the circular road structures like loops and peripheriques, as being empty and conditional only to the hierarchies of rational, inherited structures, where everything, as he says, "merely takes up their abode"—and that such emptiness and blankness is not the receptor to the lived actions or perceptions of the urban populace.

GS I see. So that's why when I visit and I am all the time driving around the city, the leftover spaces and vague fields of stuff are the result of inconsistent planning and regional fluctuations of development?

DA Yeah. That's why I also think that you have to see those spaces as part of—and again I'll refer to Lefebvre—an in-between or illusory space—you know, a space not purely visual and not purely geometrical. This kind of space is not totally synthetic, but operative as a kind of medium that identifies the confrontational aspect of each condition.

GS Perhaps this can explain why we have such a curiosity about the silence of empty parking lots or that even though we might be afraid about how everything looks the same, the strange logic of it all is perversely appealing.

DA Exactly!

GS Ignasi de Solà-Morales wrote an amazing article about the photography of the terrain vague.[3]

DA Yeah, I know it—from *Quaderns*, right? He's one of my favorite thinkers out there today!

GS Mine too. Well, as you know, then, the multiple meanings that the term *terrain vague* has in English, French, and German supply a range of possible ways to look at the metroplex, from the aquatic model (*vague* in French translates to *wave* in English) to the sort of earthy one—plus, I remember him talking about the kind of affection we have for these lost or leftover spaces that aren't used in the city but are still a part of it.

DA Right, right, but the thing that's different here, though, as opposed to the discarded urban wastelands that Solà-Morales was concerned with, is the idea that the whole city is vague terrain, you know—continuous. In fact, the liquefaction of space and the flows of capital, desire, moral judgments, discipline, knowledge, etc., have disabled the architect's ability to judge this field. That's also why we get obsessed with it—we can't really make definitive statements anymore about the form of the city. That's why we've turned to processual models rather than fixed models.

GS You seem to really like that American cities defy logical explanation.

DA Strangely, yes, because the crisis of the city sponsors the crisis of form and representation. I mean, when I look at Smithson's work, Shad Woods at Free University Berlin, Friedman, parametrics, and all that 1960s stuff, I realize that the ground on which the city is described today was inadvertently plowed up by those field megastructures attempting to be organized around artificially organic models. The struggle was obvious for the humanist but modernist apparatus making work of Team X...how do you go about building the phenomenon of the city into architecture?

GS Well, if the city is about life, you can install programmatic intensities into it, but if the city is about vagueness, then it seems as if architecture has sustained a loss of control in articulating space, because the city is so inarticulate.

DA See, that's the dilemma! Dealing with a medium that is, on the one hand, all that the city is made up of, but on the other, having to excavate new performances for it so that it doesn't just take up its place, as Lefebvre would say.

GS I think of an architect like Toyo Ito when it comes to expressing the city in building. Of course, Ito talks about Tokyo through ideas like Saran Wrap city, nomad women, the city as a garden of microchips, buildings as media ships...he seems to gather a kind of dualism to his work. It is a complete and perfect mirror of the way we live in the city, but at the same time his stuff is see-through, kind of ghostly.

DA Yeah, good point. He deals with the city with a firmly material practice but in such a way that you don't think he's even doing architecture!

GS It's like, maybe we could see the people if architecture would only get out of the way!

[1] Cf. "The Glaucous Paradise," 48.

[2] Henri Lefebvre, *The Production of Space* (Cambridge, MA: Blackwell, 1991), 296–297.

[3] Ignasi de Solà-Morales, "Terrain Vague," *Quaderns d'arquitectura i urbanisme* (1996): no. 212, 34.

Pacific East: Los Angeles

I

Los Angeles has its beauty, though like the facial makeover, it wears thin as it is exposed to our inspection.

II

Realism doesn't seem to exist in Los Angeles, except when cataclysm reminds us of it—and even then, the event-spectacle surprises us with how easily it is captured by the media.

III

To feel the sublime in Los Angeles, we must look beyond the world in front of us to the glaucous paradise constructed inside our own head.

IV

If a car is a wreck, then even the most beautiful driver is seen through the filter of ugliness.

V

Architecture's last breath in the West is the lifeguard tower. After a five-thousand-mile swim, it emerges in Tokyo as a fifty-story tower.

VI

The thing about palm trees is that they try so hard to be like other trees, but in the end they exist as icons of splendor rather than as devices of nature.

VII

In the ski slopes and golf courses of Southern California are the geometries of pleasure and frustration, a mixture likely to be matched only in the privacy of the bedroom.

VIII

Lost on most visitors to Los Angeles is the fact that it is a city, not a plastic prop waiting to be destroyed by the cynicism of the uninitiated.

IX

The terrifying possibility of an 8.0 earthquake does not rival the fear of a Hollywood bomb.

X

Buildings in Los Angeles take on the aura of history when they are renovated for the third time.

Air-Cleaning Machines

For every ficus tree in a dentist's waiting room, for every snake plant on a kitchen windowsill, for every palm tree in an office building atrium, small amounts of air molecules are cleansed through the photosynthetic action of light conversion. Engaged in a machinic process, each green plant performs a small task within the larger systems of ecology that make up the natural and artificial world. Think of every office building atrium as an enviro-mechanical system working to freshen the dead air of an elevator lobby on the eighth floor. One still suspects, however, that despite the bio-mechanical effects of green systems, nature as we make it is most often deployed to make the landscape visually pleasant.[1] The developer amortizes the cost of building a green atrium against the amenity that raises lease rates. Clearly, the pleasure performance is more efficient than the air-cleaning one.

Cover-Up

Why do so many buildings have green perimeters at the base? One rarely sees how a building engages with the terrain because of the mask of hedges, trees, flowerbeds, etc. The reason must be that architects have not considered this condition closely or that it is always assumed that, at the ground level, green is more pleasant than the surface of the building itself, as if architecture could never be as beautiful as the nature against which it presumably stands. The humor of a twenty-story extruded building with a small green base attests to our lack of success in conceiving buildings as a photosynthetic merger of hard and soft systems.[2]

Photosynthesis.[3]

[1] The "beautification" programs sponsored by CalTrans Los Angeles include heavy planting along the freeway corridors of the city. Built-in watering systems keep these green surfaces active as air cleaners, noise reducers, and pleasurizers. Given the tremendous amount of time daily commuters use the freeway system (400,000 cars per day on the 405 San Diego Freeway), these spaces become a new form of public park.

[2] See Reyner Banham, *The Architecture of the Well-tempered Environment* (London: Architectural Press, 1969, 268-270) for a description of the Olivetti Factory in Merlo, Argentina, 1963. Marco Zanuso's design incorporated precast plenums/beams with air-handling units attached to the ends of the plenums.

[3] Photosynthesis means "putting together with light." It is the process by which green plants and other organisms (bacteria) transform light energy into chemical energy. Light energy is used in plants to convert water, carbon dioxide, and minerals into oxygen and energy-rich organic compounds.

The process of photosynthesis maintains life on earth, in that all living organisms derive food (either directly or indirectly) from organic compounds formed during this process. Without it, there would be virtually no oxygen on the planet. The only organisms that can exist without it are chemosynthetic bacteria, which utilize the chemical energy of inorganic compounds.

The study of photosynthesis was begun in 1771 by Joseph Priestly, who discovered by placing a sprig of mint in a jar with a with a burned-out candle that after several days the plant had produced "a substance" that permitted the reignition of the candle. This substance was discovered to be oxygen, and in 1845 oxygen was found to form at the expense of carbon dioxide. It was discovered that light energy from the sun is stored as chemical energy in products formed during photosynthesis. Much of the complex information we now have concerning the processes involved in photosynthesis has been developed since the 1950s. Investigation into photosynthesis still continues, aided by the use of radioactive isotopes and fluorescence techniques and by the study of photosynthetic bacteria and algae.

The process of photosynthesis most likely evolved from simple colored molecules called *pigments*, such as the chlorophylls of green plants, bacteriophyll of photosynthetic bacteria, hemin (the red pigment of blood), and cytochromes, a group of pigment molecules essential in photosynthesis and cellular respiration. These primitive colored cells had to evolve mechanisms for using the light energy absorbed by their pigments. The first oxygenic (oxygen-producing) cells were probably cyanophytes—blue-green algae—which appeared two to three billion years ago. These are believed to have greatly increased the oxygen content of the atmosphere, making it possible for the development of aerobic (oxygen-using) organisms.

In chemical terms, photosynthesis is a light-energized oxidation-reduction process (oxidation refers to the removal of electrons from a molecule, reduction to gain). The energy of light is used to drive the oxidation of water (H_2O) to produce oxygen gas (O_2), hydrogen ions ($H+$), and electrons. Most of the hydrogen ions and removed electrons are transferred to carbon dioxide (CO_2), which is reduced to organic products. Other electrons and hydrogen ions are used to reduce nitrate and sulfate to amino and sulfhydryl groups in amino acids, the building blocks of protein. The major products in most green cells are carbohydrates (starch and sugar sucrose). Carbohydrate production occurs according to the following formula:

$$CO_2 + 2H_2O + (CH_2O) + O_2 + H_2O$$

Amino acids, proteins, lipids (fats), pigments, and other organic compounds of green tissues are also synthesized during photosynthesis.

Photosynthesis occurs in two stages. The first is the light stage, in which the photochemical reactions take place; the second is the dark phase, during which purely chemical reactions take place, controlled by enzymes. Stage 1 produces ATP (adenosine triphosphate) and NADPH (nicotine adenine dinucleotide phosphate), which are used to reduce the CO_2 to organic compounds in a process called *carbon fixation* in Stage 2.

The shorter the wavelength of light, the greater the energy (blue light thus has more energy than red). The energy used in photosynthesis can be estimated at 450 kilocalories per mole (6.02 x 1023 molecules) of oxygen evolved. In general, a total storage of 1 percent of the energy received in the dry biomass of an agricultural crop over one year would be an exceptional yield. Although the maximum storage possible if the photosynthetic process were carried out an optimal level is around 30 percent, this yield is never reached because of numerous factors — only during certain months can sunlight be absorbed; some energy is needed to drive the processes that keep the plant alive; photosynthesis is sometimes slowed down by an excess in production of sugars and starches, etc.

Photosynthesis occurs entirely within the chloroplasts, which form a particular portion of each cell. Chlorophylls are the main light-absorbing molecules in green plants, but other pigments such as carotenes and carotenoids (the orange-yellow color found in carrots) can also absorb light. However, the energy must be passed to chlorophyll before conversion can occur.

The most important factors affecting the rate of photosynthesis in plants are the amount of light, carbon dioxide supply, temperature, water supply, and availability of minerals. The rate is also determined by plant health, maturity, and whether or not it is in flower. Increasing the amount of carbon dioxide directly increases plant photosynthesis, as does a rise in temperature, provoked itself by a rise in CO_2 in the atmosphere.

Smog Monster

On July 11, 1997, the South Coast Air Quality Management District (AQMD) of California adopted a regulation that constitutes one of the largest reductions ever in hydrocarbon emissions by requiring businesses to switch from petroleum-based to water-based degreasing solvents. More precisely, it is the single largest hydrocarbons emissions reduction measure adopted in eight years. The measure will reduce volatile organic compounds (VOC) from solvent degreasing tanks by 76 percent or 40.2 tons per day by 2010.

The AQMD attack is logical, as solvent use is one of the largest sources of smog-forming VOC emissions in Southern California, equal to the combined emissions from every gas station, oil refinery, petroleum storage facility, and gasoline tank truck in the region.

Smog is produced when the following elements work together in a chemical fusion:
— Sunlight
— The production of oxides of nitrogen (NO^x)
— The production of volatile organic compounds (VOCs)
— A temperature greater than 18°C
When the word *smog* was coined in London earlier in this century, it was formed clearly from a contraction of the words *(coal) smoke* and *fog*. Yet, when one looks at the chemical makeup of smog today, the element of fog (a cloudlike mass or layer of minute water droplets or ice crystals near the surface of the earth, appreciably reducing visibility) is not part of the equation. As light and heat meet volatile chemicals, smoke is more likely to be invoked as the dominant (and only) operative in this pair of climatological phenomena. Hardly twins, smoke and fog emerge from vastly different places; one is the product of deliberate conditions orchestrated in the industrial world, the other of seemingly benign weather patterns. Seen as vague, evanescent vapors, however, they become much more reflective of one another. Yet, why assign nature (fog) an accomplice role in the horror of polluted skies? Is it because fog or marine layers collide with the industrial world in a way that, rather than diluting the chemical haze, actually turns it into something much more unhealthy?

If ecology is the branch of biology dealing with the relations between organisms and their environments, then smog is a primary example of how these relations are made more and more complex in our technologically advancing world. Smog is, in fact, a defining condition of ecology itself, one that sets out to reassign culpability in the crisis of the environment. Because the overwhelming beauty of the (found?) landscape and the forces that shape it (all sublime and dangerous) intersect with the built environment in ways not always productive, the hazards of the environment may themselves be products of a collaboration of natural and technical conditions that require a new "politics of convergence" instead of the prevailing one of antagonism.

The AQMD resolution does not, it seems, affect architecture. The reduction of toxic chemicals in the environment is indeed essential to the scrubbing down of the skies. However, this is not a spatial or material reduction (as in the reduction of sprawl, which would reduce auto emissions). It is simply the most effective change (so far) that has been implemented in repairing the environment and it has little to do with form or the built environment. It may further suggest that the complex relationship between the industrial landscape and the human is not made problematic so much by architecture as by the chemicalscapes around us. Of course, this does not abrogate our responsibility as architects to consider how our buildings affect the landscape. Whether urban, artificial, digital, or natural, the issue of form as a devastating condition in our various ecologies should not be ballasted by the idea that architecture is a loss-incurring enter-prise fraught with destruction from the outset. The AQMD resolution points to the supple relations between the politics of production and the spatializing of human inhabitation.

Beach View/Dealey Plaza

Where the identities of New York and Chicago turn on the morphological distinctions of their respective architectures, the similitudinal condition of the typical North American city leaves Los Angeles to create an image different from Detroit, Dallas, Atlanta, or Phoenix through other means. The mediated visual field ceaselessly projects the scenography of Los Angeles, thereby ensuring its limitless expansion, and transmutes local interest into cultural axiom.

In today's world, it is the particularity of *image* and *event* that begins to separate cities, in the process creating identities more powerful than any skyline.

Pacific West: Japan

1 Shibuya

The new mountain ranges of the urban mass of Tokyo were created because of two great twentieth-century tragedies: the Kanto earthquake of 1923 and the bombing of World War II. Tokyo is the oldest new city in the world, where a precise, hyper-crafted series of scapes has arisen out of an older order. Shibuya is a contemporary shopping machine with the labyrinthine pattern of an ancient hilltown.

2 Four Minutes

The precision of the train arrivals in the Tokyo subway system is astonishing. Large, intricate sheets of train intervals are located in every station, each a matrix of time and place whose information is perhaps the most descriptive index of the city. Every four minutes the train is there.

3 Melancholy

With the collapse of the bubble economy in March 1991, Tokyo became a normal place, quite different from the world of limitless distractions and the unending flow of money. The action in the city is below the surface of the spectacle of urban form—it is found instead in the minor conditions of late-night beef bowls and pachinko parlors.

4 Dashboard

The smooth, new contours of the Japanese automobile are everywhere. Old, dented, or even dirty cars simply do not exist in Japan, and no one keeps a car longer than three or four years. One wonders where all the used cars go.

5 Expediency

The take-out bento box is but a diagram for a larger form of immediate consumption that structures the contemporary landscape of Japan. Combining an overwhelming desire to be quick and efficient with a highly technological infrastructure, it is possible for food, ideas, and fashions to be processed at lightning speeds.

6 Claustrophobia

The scale of built space in Japan seems to be that of a semi-miniaturized world where a six-tatami mat room is quite large. The limits of space create ergonomic relationships that are much more intimate than those in the West. When miniaturized technology is turned on this spatially imploded world, the city seems to deepen in a virtual sense as cameras and monitors supply new apertures of escape into another world, a distorted replica of the first.

7 Automatic Doors

White cloth seat covers, white gloves on the driver, automatically opening and closing doors... A taxi ride across Tokyo may take hours, so at least one can be late for meetings in style.

8 Night

When night falls in Tokyo, the air becomes colorized, full of life, injected with the hues of a million billboards. The light of the moon is always eclipsed by the overwhelming glow of the landscape of signforms.

9 Tradition

The Japanese rebuild Ise Shrine every twenty years. Conventional wisdom regarding history says that everything is bound to event and artifacts, but it seems that the Japanese, every time the structure is rebuilt, remind us that the object doesn't mean as much as the code of its own origin—we don't ask how old the wood is, we look into the meaning that it carries.

10 Building Typology

Since 1960, the value of land has escalated so sharply in Tokyo (and most of Japan) that what were formerly large blocks of land are now striated bands of increasingly narrower plots, as the larger plots proved to be too expensive to buy for most. Out of this new pattern of economic parcelization has emerged a variety of sliver building types, usually eight to ten stories tall.

11 Urban Dynamics

Everyone is a blur here, moving together as a mass of popular flows. Near and far, across every urban square, the homogeneity of culture renders the masses as a bulwark of corporate movement, blended together into a seamless structure of desire.

12 Uniform Culture

Without putting too critical a point on it, Japan's is a "uniform" culture. It is only after business hours that youth culture and the transformation of the young office lady from uniformed tea server to super-hot Roppongi girl begins to dismantle the sterility of life—it's possible to see the binary even in the concept of personal identity. There's no schizophrenia here, just another structure!

13 Coherent Chaos

In contrast to Los Angeles, a city built out of endless grids, fluid infrastructure, and seemingly devoid of traditional urbanism, Tokyo is the opposite, where all the urban references are played out rather clearly through intense building mass, requisite monuments, neighborhoods, effective mass transportation, and teeming masses of people.

14 Mirror

Tokyo is a mediated imagescape so fraught with confusion as to the first degree of reality or nature that one is left to make architecture here that is a reflection of these mediated systems. Doing this proves that the indigenous spatial ideas of Tokyo at the end of the twentieth century are simply a set of conceptual mirrors or surfaces reflecting contemporary conditions. Was Warhol right when he said that all the best ideas are on TV?

15 Everything

In Akihabara, the concept of everything becomes clear. Anything automated or electronic may be found there. With a great void at the center of Tokyo, it seems as if everything that could be powerful has been poured into this electronic paradise of the city.

Ryoan-ji Zen Garden, Kyoto

Fifteen stones in three constellations/islands/groups/accumulations floating within a sea/field/liquid/plane of miniature white stones/gravel/pebbles/sand. Groups of three, five, and seven stones.

The question is: Why are the stones there? Of course, to even ask *why* is to acknowledge the Western affliction of reason. My eyes go to the stones because they are different from the gravel, because they have form, because they are an event. I keep looking at them. They ground my gaze and become unwanted ballasts. It is impossible to rid my view of them. Zen philosophy tells me, "Look between the stones." It makes me think, what *is* the sound of one hand clapping? Stop thinking. I can't. I keep thinking about *The Problem of Form*.[1]

Beyond the walls, the green landscape is borrowed. Why? How? Is nature flattened, a kind of two-dimensional mapping at the edge of the space? Is it the opposite, the reminder of depth? Is it borrowed to dramatize the affected geometries and gradients of the garden? One response, a heretical one: the borrowed landscape is not the nature beyond the walls but the stones themselves. They should not be there, but they have been borrowed as a reference to binary thinking. What could this unknown garden designer have been thinking? If the stones weren't there, wouldn't the whole site be conceptually infinite and monological (all gravel)?

Preliminary response: Perhaps I should just conclude that the stones are merely larger versions of the gravel—not any different, just bigger.

Final response: I am convinced that the stones are not there when I am not looking at them. In this site, geometry is not independent of experience. Maybe by rejecting Kant and pretty much everyone else, I could imagine the stones away.[2] When I return again, I can only hope that they will reappear.

[1] See Adolph von Hildebrand, *The Problem of Form*, trans. Max Meyer and Robert Morris Ogden (New York: Stechert, 1907). This seminal book introduced the concept of the uninterrupted continuum as a spatial plasma where distant and close views of form contribute to a relativizing of form—that is, that material form is not a fixed material essence when connected to perception and disconnected from physics. Paul Rotterdam, an Austrian expatriate artist teaching at Harvard whose art theory seminar I took in 1980, based much of his position on von Hildebrand's text. Refer also to Sanford Kwinter's equally seminal article "La Citta Nuova: Modernity and Continuity," *Zone 1/2: The City* (New York: Zone Books, 1986). Kwinter quotes this passage from von Hildebrand, which is applicable here: "Let us imagine total space (*das Raumganze*) as a body of water, into which we may sink certain vessels, and thus be able to define individual volumes of water without however destroying the idea of a continuous mass of water enveloping all," 89. After von Hildebrand, Alois Riegl further developed the idea that human perception is fatefully linked to architectural production. He developed, in fact, "the concept of *Kunstwollen*, or artistic will, determining that works of art were such not by virtue of their technical or geographical conditions or by the materials from which they were constructed, as Semper had thought, but as the products of will—a subjective desire to manifest a vision of the world not through symbols or images but by means of new and changing spatial experiences." Ignasi de Solà-Morales, *Differences*, trans. Graham Thompson, ed. Sarah Whiting (Cambridge, MA: MIT Press, 1997), 95.

[2] Clearly this relates to the famous story where one scientist asks another, "Do you really think the moon isn't there when you aren't looking at it?" Because I cannot enter Ryoan-ji and walk on the gravel, reach out and touch the stones, or run my hand over the bounding walls, feeling history and time being quietly sucked into the microcrevices, I can only see what I think I see. I must dismiss the possibility of knowing the world through touch at that moment. Without touch, mere vision is suspect, as Bertrand Russell suggests when he reminds us that "Macbeth's dagger was unreal because it was not sensible to feeling as to sight." *The ABC of Relativity* (New York: Mentor Books, 1969), 10. But if I am to think about space, perception, and what I see from the *genkan* (veranda) of Ryoan-ji, I think that even though I cannot verify the material factuality of the stones, I can, as the *Kunstwollen* suggests, will the stones into place and have faith that they are there.

AIR   GLASS   POWER   WATER   ARCHITECTURE

Night view from swimming pool deck

Massey Residence (Schnitt-Haus)

Project No. 9405
Los Angeles, California
1994

The Endless Grid

When one meditates on the endless fields of postwar housing in Los Angeles, the conditions of urbanism there that are reflected in the astonishing density of any given neighborhood grid become apparent, even when this coverage is but one or two stories high. In most areas dwellings are just a few meters apart; this repetitious fabric can only be described as machinic, relentlessly repeated floor plans with little concern for solar orientation or spatial experimentation. These cellular structures have supported most cultural aspirations for an architecture of both familiar domestic iconography and functioning privacy.

This brief interrogation into the basic performative deficiencies of the Los Angeles housing grid—which itself must be distinguished from newer peripheral suburban developments of Southern California, if only by fifty years of maturing artificial nature—should not, however, eclipse the more welcome aspects of individual ownership and minor forms of territorial sovereignty as reflected in the back yard. This only suggests what most architects have long argued for, especially through the Case Study Program—that the house should be more responsive to both local and phenomenal conditions than the market delivers.

If uniformity can be both sublime and stifling, then the problem of designing a house in this milieu is to match the best aspects of the suburban field with those variations and deformations of the limits normally placed on a basic house. Recognizing this problem and its attendant, potentially transformative solutions, the client asked that a straightforward three-bedroom, two-bath program for the house become a new spatial experience within the grid and that we resist the temptation to use the grid as a ground for difference.

Sections, Not Plans

What emerged from this mandate was a strategy focused on the sectional development of the house while leaving the site plan to be shaped by the forces of normal setbacks and outdoor programs such as a swimming pool and yard. Thus, the house is positioned on the site like the other houses in the context are, so it does not assert difference through this means. Designed for a site 50 x 150 feet, a slightly larger version of typical postwar planning grids, the house is set back 40 feet from the curb, leaving 70 feet for the rear yard.

In section, the house sits in a concrete excavation with the driveway sloping from grade to minus 9 feet to accommodate parking underneath the main public space of the house. Given that the house explores section over plan, the program is deployed over seven split levels, a move intended to spatially striate the program into interlocking zones of specific uses. By lowering the structure into the site, a 29-foot-high (three-story) house is seen as a two-level house. The experience and concept of the house then, is about the section cut. The front and rear elevations show the roof skin and the basic extruded form of the overall volume. Inside, the circulation space revolves around a stair that connects the different levels, each one shifted in height to create half-levels and splintered views of adjacent spaces.

This new domestic terrain is arbitrated by the owner's movements. The owner is an inexhaustible traveler through the pathways of cultural production. Within an urban milieu that is the subject of countless rehearsals of both angst and ennui, this house sits as an ambivalent figure, committed to the preservation of site typology while internally engaging in an extreme criticism of architectural similitudes. The living experience exposes the tectonic and constructional aspects of the house and allows the inhabitant to be in the space being formed as well as to see the shearing effect caused by the stepped floor plates. Exposed galvanized steel structural systems explain the building's internal logic.

Structural Premise

Two main structural systems are at work in the house:
— Above the garage, the main floor of the house is supported by a discreet steel assembly that rests on smaller splayed columns and a concrete storage wall. Across the entrance space, the kitchen, dining, and work areas sit on a concrete excavation.
— Two large structural bents in a rounded V-shape in section support the roof. Running perpendicular to these elements are purlins that stiffen the frame. The bedrooms are essentially suspended from the structural bents, reducing the number of columns in the building.

Tommy Newsom is, well, not an impeccable dresser. Tonight he has on a real tie, but he's wearing a clip-on suit.
—Johnny Carson, c. 1975, *Tonight Show* monolog.

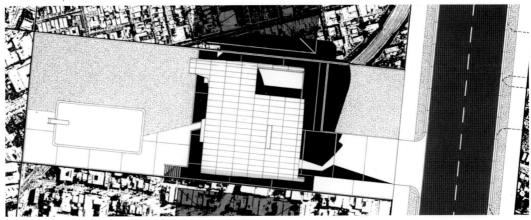

Site plan

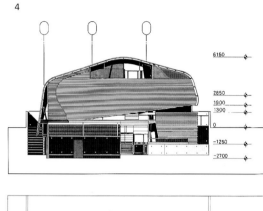

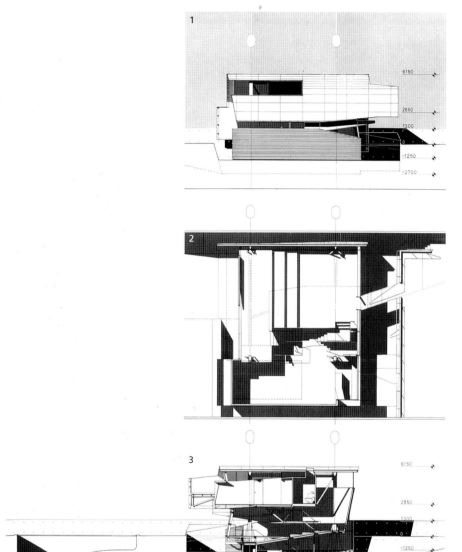

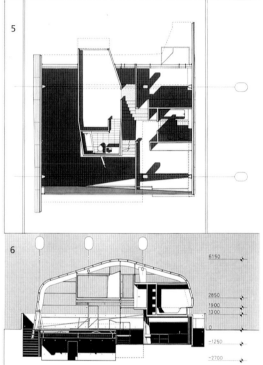

1 West elevation
2 Second floor plan
3 Longitudinal section

4 North elevation
5 Third floor plan
6 Cross section

Aerial view from the northwest

North elevation: view from the street

AIR CONDITIONING   WEED EATERS   MARKET RESEARCH   NINTENDO   THE VALLEY   POLICE HELICOPTERS   LAX   GASOLINE STAINS

SUN   SKIN   SURF   SPRAWL

MASSEY
9405.2a
WEST LOS ANGELES, CA.

View into entrance from carport

71

If technology is latent with purpose, then any problems revolving around its architectural use might take on a value which is inherent in the object and suggestively engagable b

⚠ *geometry*

9861-8743-930001.87 DIT.9X

CHLORINATED AIR   HALOGEN BUZZ

OSCULATIONS

MASSEY
9405.2a
WEST LOS ANGELES, CA
a. waisler 11
cor-tex

PROJECTNUMBER

COMPUTER
PROFILING

© 1994 COR-TEX / NEIL M. DENARI
1996 COR-TEX STRATOGRAPHICS
PRINTED IN THE USA by   eclipse

CLIENT: Richard Massey

LOCATION

FRAME NUMBER

ARCHITECT: Neil M. Denari

Detail of south elevation

View toward kitchen and dining area from living space

View from dining area across living space

Structural x-ray 1

All structural elements are galvanized steel with bolted and welded connections

main structural beams

intermediate glazing structure

tapered column w/struts

main floor structure

aluminum glazing system

cast concrete foundation and bearing walls

MASSEY
9405 2a
WEST LOS ANGELES CA
washer S3

X-RAY

Structural x-ray 2

Sectional perspective view

Project No. 9307
Central Glass Ideas Competition
Los Angeles, California
1993

The Overlit Realm

Over our lives preside the great twin leitmotifs of the 20th century—sex and paranoia....The main "fact" of the 20th century is the concept of the unlimited possibility. This predicate of science and technology enshrines the notion of a moratorium on the past, the irrelevancy and even the death of the past, and the limitless alternatives available to the present. What links the first flight of the Wright brothers to the invention of the Pill is the social and sexual philosophy of the ejector seat. From J.G. Ballard's famous introduction, often quoted, to the novel *Crash* (1973).

Rainforest of the Mind

To introduce this project with such provocative and now politically troublesome words, filled with Ballard's clarion call to the realities of excess, the death of affect, and the analgesics of the present, is to acknowledge the convulsive forces at work in the twentieth century. What makes Ballard's words so simultaneously heraldic and cautionary is that what was once thought to be unlimited—that is, the natural resources of ideas and the materials to forge them—is now a landscape of depletion. While Ballard points to the proliferation of science and technology around us, he refers to the unmatched and always expanding human imagination as unlimited. At the end of the century, the once positive processes of *idea to production* and *concept to implementation* have become adversaries in the crisis of limits. With virtually a complete history of the last hundred years now available to us, and with Ballard's assessment of the first three quarters of it against which to measure the last quadrant, the sprawling and exponentially more complex curves of the tumultuous avenues of progress chart a riveting graph of events.

Doubt

The competition brief asked a series of simple questions about one hundred years of complexity: How does one design a museum of an entire century? What will go inside it? Where will it be? How large will it need to be? Looking back on it, impossibility should have prevailed, a white sheet of paper submitted as the ultimate schema of refusal. Instead, with the obstinacy of architecture in hand, the project proceeded with these premises:
— Given Einstein's famous phrase "God does not play dice" and Gödel's theory of incompleteness (welded to Heisenberg's uncertainty principle) as scientific and ethical opposites, the twentieth century will be remembered for its movement past Newtonian dynamics into an even more chaotic conflict of relative, indeterminate conditions.
— The invention of the airplane completed a centuries-old series of meditations on the possibility of humans overcoming the force of gravity. Since 1901, humans have been liberated from the ground by aircraft, leaving behind the weight and monumentality of the preceding centuries.
— But since 1945, with the advent of nuclear weaponry, science and technology's politics has carried with it an ominous sense of liberation wholly different from that of flight. Nagasaki began a program of nature harnessed so powerfully that today's environmental irresponsibility may well lead back to political responsibility.

Site

Los Angeles International Airport (LAX) was chosen as a site for more than obvious reasons. First, it is a program that exists around the world, one where each day more than five hundred flights are a reminder that 400,000 pounds can leap through the air. Second, Los Angeles is at the edge of the West, perhaps the final frontier, geographically, of this century. If any city could contain the history of the twentieth century, it is Los Angeles—a city that is a cross section of the last hundred years.

The museum is located east of Terminal 1 at LAX on a site approximately 1,000 feet x 900 feet.

Grids versus Blobs

The scheme is simple and obviously dialectical. A system of Cartesian pathways of circulation connect ten cloudforms, each dedicated to the exhibition of a single decade of events through the display of artifacts and images. The circulation grid is deterministic and precise, whereas the clouds are vague and nonobjective, an ordered lattice placed between bubble chambers of atomic movement. The twentieth century has moved from Newtonian clockwork logic to open-ended illogics and from terrestrial imprisonment to supersonic and orbital flight.

So, as the century closes, we again, much humbler and wiser, return to the ground to study the effects of our own progress. At the end, the building for the final decade of the century emerges from the ground only to be connected again to a raised artificial groundplane that refers to our need to study nature in a new way.

Does this mean that (sex + paranoia) x (flight / quantum physics) = 20th century?

Top Interior perspective view of 1920–1929 Building
Bottom Airplane interior

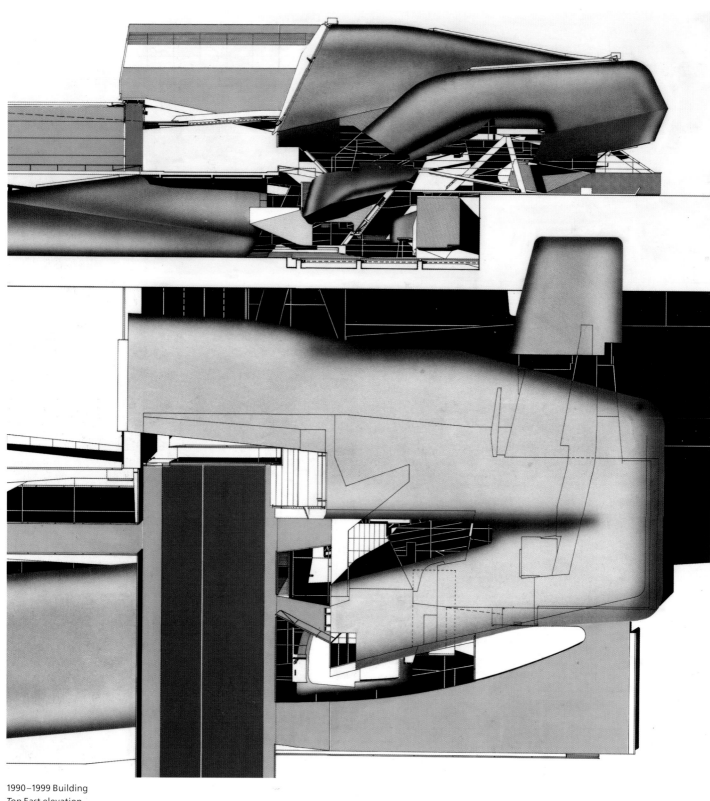

1990–1999 Building
Top East elevation
Bottom Roof plan

Top Section through 1940–1949 Building
Bottom Site plan

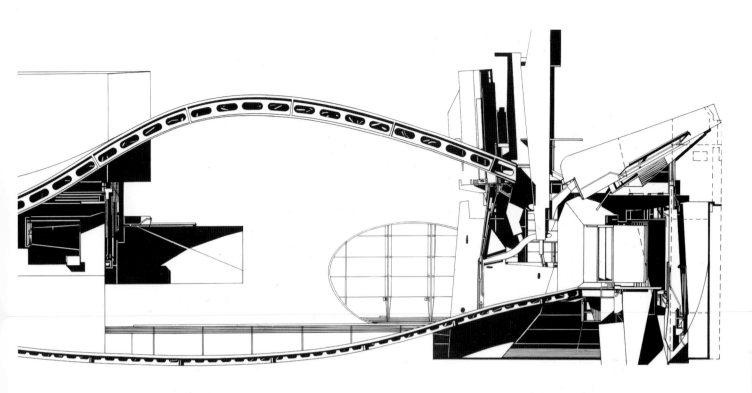

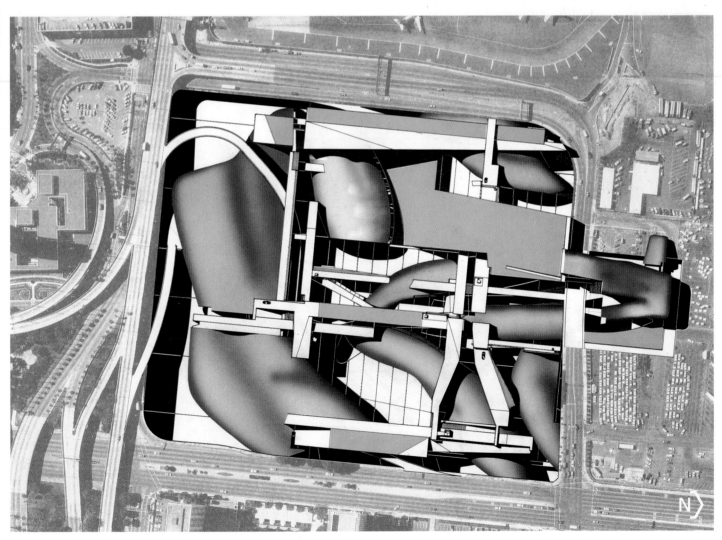

Vertical Smoothouse

Project No. 9704
Los Angeles, California
1997

Land Value: Astronomical
The site is located in a residential neighborhood where four-level apartment buildings and one-level single-family houses are adjacent to one another, mediated by green landscapes of domestic nature. With a recent and, indeed, precipitous rise in real estate values in this area of Los Angeles, the client wished to study the possible strategies to increase the value of the land and the size of the existing house (150 square meters) by building vertically above the footprint of the adjacent but detached two-car garage. A variance for parking allows just a single automobile to be parked underneath the second and third floors of the new house, leaving a multipurpose space and bathroom on the ground floor, easily accessible to the existing house across a small patio space.

The middle floor contains an efficiency kitchen, dining space, and an exterior deck on the north side of the new vertical project. The top floor contains a bathroom and an open space for living, working, or sleeping.

Mono-skin: Localized Worldsheet
Geometrically, the house is formed by a single curving sheet that describes the basic envelope of the house. The sheet bends into itself, creating invelopes or internal surfaces that merge seamlessly with the exterior. In attempting to force the monological condition of the Klein Bottle (that only a single surface describes the object) into a two-dimensional sheet, the house necessarily must return to a binary condition of inside and outside in order to carry the possibility of continuousness. This persistence of surface is activated by the performance of the envelope-invelope in that the radii never allow a corner or edge to articulate the limits of typical Cartesian geometry. A structural steel frame supports the sheet and is hidden within an outer layer of standing seam galvanized steel sheet and an inner layer of gypsum drywall.

The worldsheet here performs in specifically localized ways. On each side of the house, the envelope reacts to the conditions it faces, whether more open to the adjacent house of the owners or more closed on the west side, where the proximity of the neighboring house as well as the low, direct light of late afternoon sun are invasive factors that need to be resisted.

Cover-Up
Finally, a texturemapped [texturemapping is a new computer graphic technique] surface of flowers is proposed as a supergraphical mirroring operation and as the final skin of the house (see page 4). The field of artificial environments known to be manifest as front yards, gardens, swimming pools, etc., is reflected and, indeed, enlarged as the iconography of the pleasurized landscape. As a modus operandi not of irony but of ecological concern, the image-graphic of nature is only one step removed from a local type of domesticated nature, itself already a kind of simulation.

Question from the audience: Why is there an obsession for the continuous, single surface?
ND: Because it's a conceptual economy of means.
Audience: What?

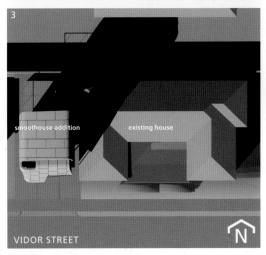

VIDOR STREET

1 Existing garage
2 Night view of existing house
3 Site plan

View into carport/entrance

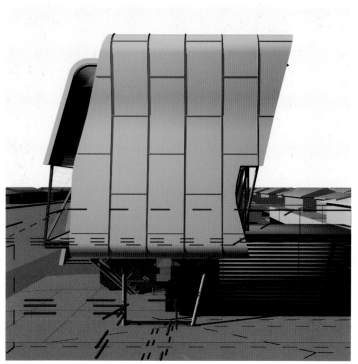

East elevation

View of southwest corner

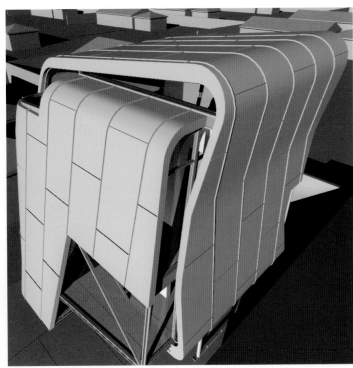

Aerial view from the southeast

Aerial view from the southwest

South elevation from the street

South elevation detail, looking up

View of north side into living room

View of stair into second floor

View of first floor bedroom

View of kitchen with stair circulation

Project No. 9803
Los Angeles, California
1998

How High?

When Le Corbusier declared that New York was not tall enough, he had not seen Los Angeles. With water all around it, Manhattan has nowhere to go but up. Questions of money and engineering are the only limits to the ultimate height of the ultimate Euclidean grid. Los Angeles on the other hand, has been asked, how wide? how far? how long? But rarely, how high?

With the Pacific Ocean containing only in one direction, Los Angeles has extended everywhere else, becoming a massive horizontal development rarely more than two stories high. Here the question of "how high" establishes not only a resistance to horizontal sprawl but also a kind of ecology of verticality in a city where density and building mass are structured by the mobility of the car and the related problems of parking.

Parking: The Inhibiting Factor

Multistory buildings in Los Angeles use unbuilt spaces as parking lots to generate return on site investment. Such buildings occur when location or programmatic density creates a performative economic logic where investment in a repetitious structure yields high profit margins. Maximum floor-area ratio is rarely reached in Los Angeles, however, as attendant codes concerning parking quite often limit the scale of building. Parking garages, therefore, become inevitable extensions of the architectural program, a necessary service buildingscape. Los Angeles architects must excavate space enough for 800 cars to support an office complex of more than 35,000 square meters.

Site

The location of this office block study is at the intersection of Pico Boulevard and the San Diego Freeway. Pico Boulevard extends from downtown Los Angeles in the east to the Santa Monica beach in the west. More than thirteen miles long, it is one of several major east-west surface streets in Los Angeles. Pico roughly parallels Interstate 10 (Santa Monica Freeway), which is less than a mile to the south. Four

miles from the ocean, the San Diego Freeway (Interstate 405) runs north-south through the west side of Los Angeles. Its more than 450,000 cars per day make it the most traveled freeway in the United States. Where Pico passes under the elevated 405, an extended void is created below the freeway between two north-south surface streets, Sawtelle and Cotner. This space is the catalyst for the site.

Located on the south side of Pico, it is a 40-meter-deep block that runs almost 350 meters in length. Even though the project is on a massive scale, the building casts shadows only over the street, not over the adjacent housing behind it.

Snowflakes

Below the San Diego Freeway, an irregular grid of oversized concrete columns interrupts a three-story-high empty space. These columns provide the vertical structure for two levels of parking slabs spanning the 40-meter space. Exploiting this "lost" space within the city not only gives a use to this emptiness but also incorporates it into a much larger building projected on either side of it. Three distinct eight-story buildings are created out of a continuous series of butt-jointed building sections. The freeway and Sawtelle Street cut into this relentless organization so as to form a six-section building and a thin one-section building on the west side of the 405 and a nine-section building on the east side. Each building section is 15 meters long and, like snowflakes, is repetitive yet different.

To accentuate the laminar structure of this large building complex, the sections are coded in a three-color pattern, repeating in the same sequence along the entire length of the building. Four floors of parking occur under the two larger building components. The typical building section has an opaque aluminum panel surface (worldsheet) perforated with windows and configured to allow for lease space and public circulation. Each section has a different formal configuration so that any deformations in its construction do not register. The facades and the interior circulation space produce a shearing effect by creating a linear montage of self-similar forms, not unlike structuralist film.

View along Pico Boulevard looking east

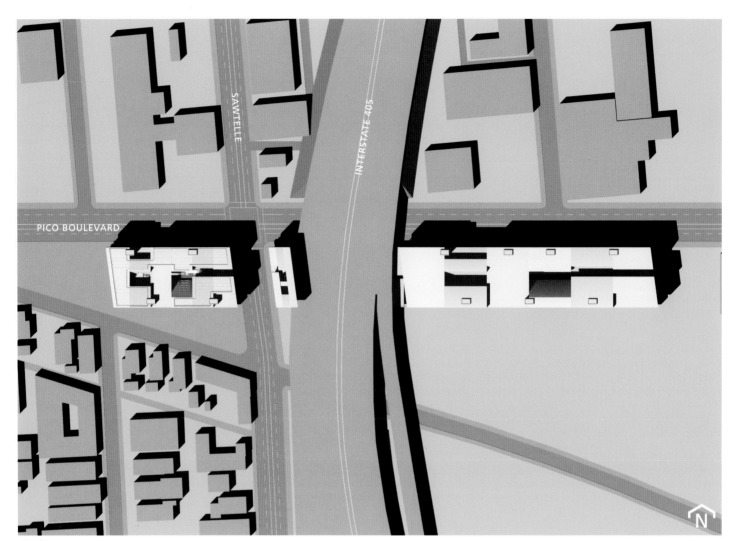

Site plan

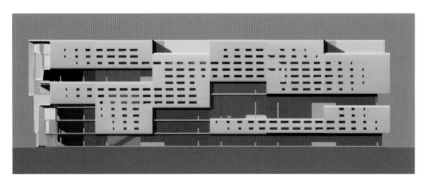

South elevation of West Building

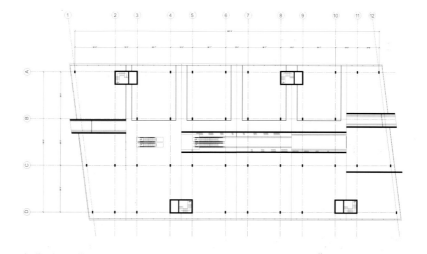

Ground floor plan   +0.00'

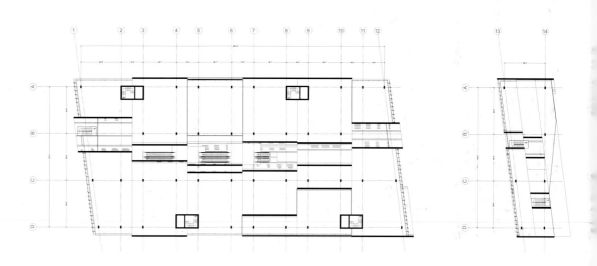

Third floor plan   +22.00'

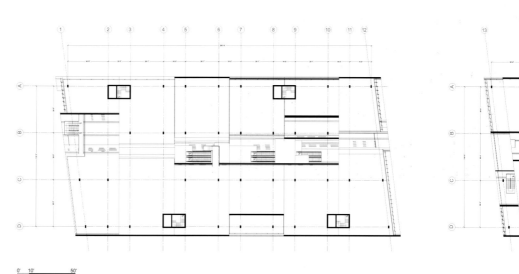

Fourth floor plan   +33.00'

Northwest view from Pico Boulevard

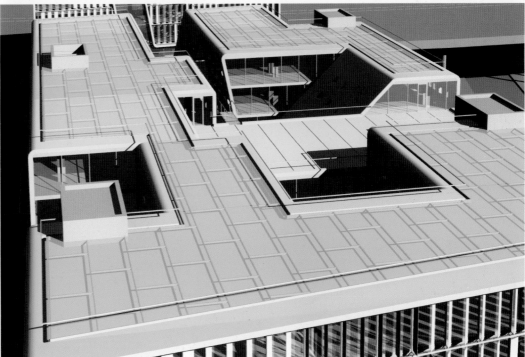

Views of roofscape looking east

Rooftop view

Views of internal circulation

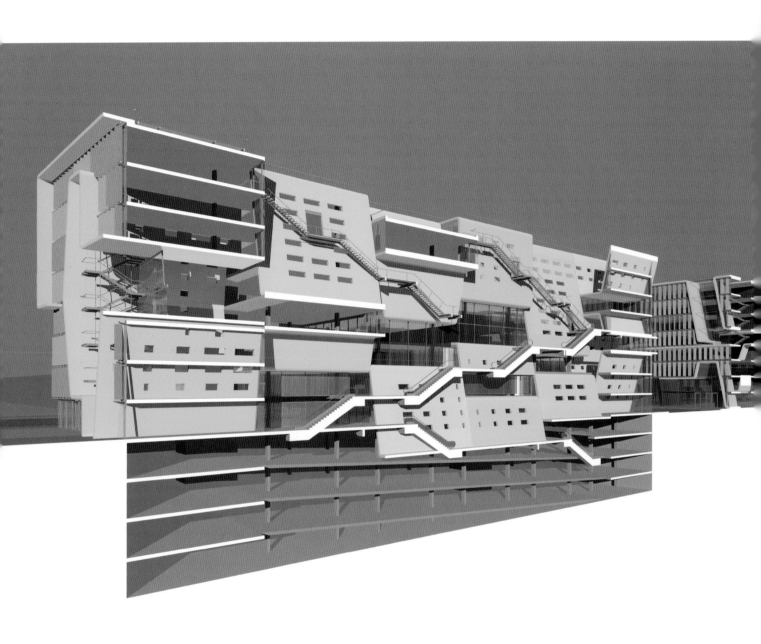

Longitudinal sectional perspective

Section A

Section B

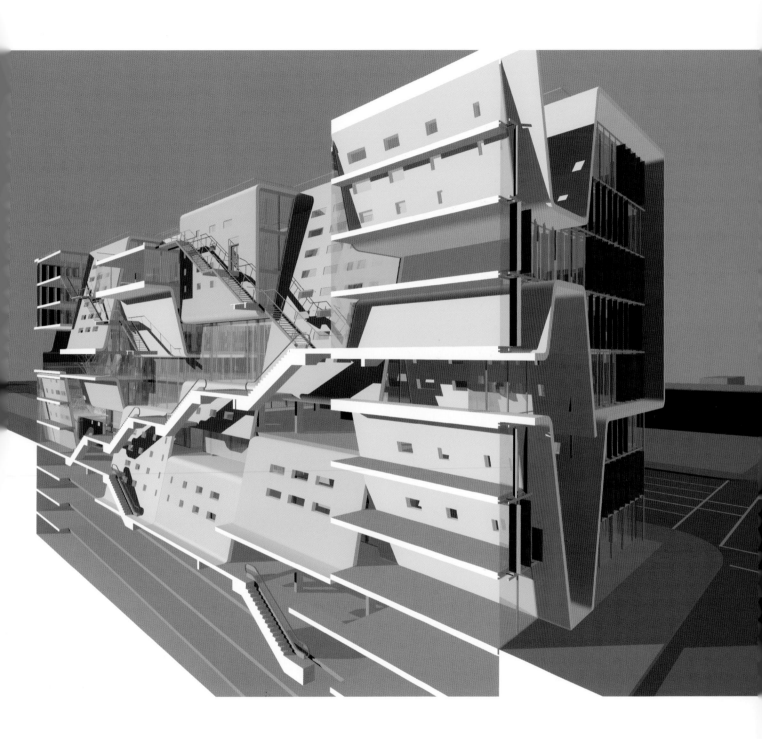

Aerial view from above Interstate 405

View of Pico-Sawtelle intersection

View looking north from Sawtelle Boulevard

Northwest view of Sliver Building

Project No. 9802
Agoura Hills, California
1998

Mergers
Los Angeles County, in the last three years, saw a major shift in the structure of large business operations through the concepts of consolidation and merger. In the aerospace and entertainment industries in particular, many corporate giants became even larger by acquiring competing companies, a strategy designed to not only diversify interests but to dominate market share. These behemoth companies, such as Boeing, Disney, and Time Warner, articulate and disperse power across vast regions of social, economic, and even political territories through sheer size. Collusion, cooptation, monopolies, mergers, institutionalizing, and so on all still seem to be operating as capitalist strategies. However, a new, more mobile scale of operations (primarily in the computer and biomedical research areas) engendered by technical knowledge more than physical size occurs in a new space freed from the heavy ballast and oppression of the corporate and the governmental. Robotics, data management, computer software, and hardware systems exist in pervasive yet often transparent layers—just more building infill—as renovated warehouses and new industrial office parks appear.

No More Golf Courses
Nearly three thousand technology-based firms exist in Los Angeles, with five hundred more predicted to be created this year. Information economies are on the rise, surely the quickest and most persistent area of revitalization in the wake of the largesse experienced in the corridors of capitalism. The physicality of land and its economic viability as investment, however, plummeted with the downturn of the early 1990s. Japanese real estate assets alone on the West Coast soared in the 1980s bubble economy to 77 billion dollars. By 1994, that figure had slumped to 46 billion dollars as Asian investors divested interests in the deflated real estate market, incurring huge losses of money and faith in California. Meanwhile, more interest in acquiring and developing information occurred across Los Angeles County, given the tremendous rise in computer sales, internet markets, and software development.

Site and Program
At the periphery of Los Angeles, near the Ventura County line, Agoura Hills has become the new Silicon Alley of Southern California. Technology-related companies and developers, particularly in biomedical fields, have begun to coalesce in this area north of Malibu. The Ventura Freeway (101) runs east-west at the southern edge of Agoura Hills and serves as the major artery for high-speed traffic along the Pacific Coast. The specific site for the building is adjacent to the freeway, with frontage road access to the 3.8-acre gently sloping site.

The program calls for a large, single building consisting of four biomedical and computer/information-based companies. Each company has office space, laboratories, conference rooms, and warehouse space, while the auditorium, cafeteria, main lobby, and health club are shared functions. To maximize the land use, parking and service vehicle access are underneath the building, which is raised one level.

Roof detail at entrance

View of entrance ramp

View into northeast quadrant

View from above freeway

Aerial view from the south

Detail of south corner

Interior view from south corner toward entry

Interior view at roof shear

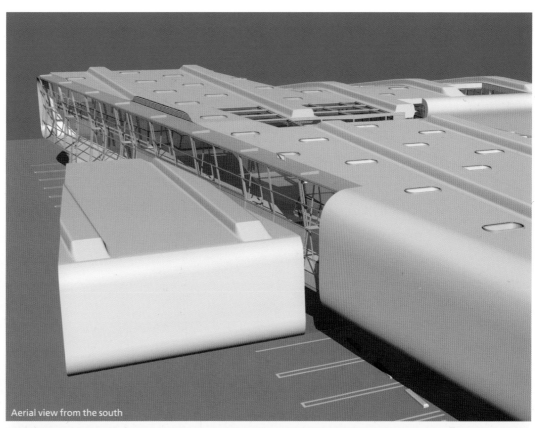

Aerial view from the south

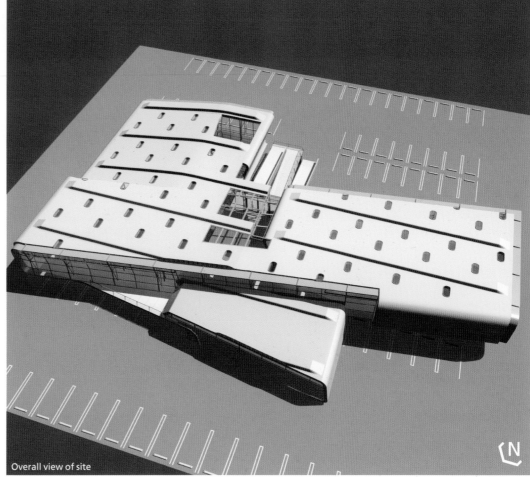

Overall view of site

Detail view of auditorium exterior

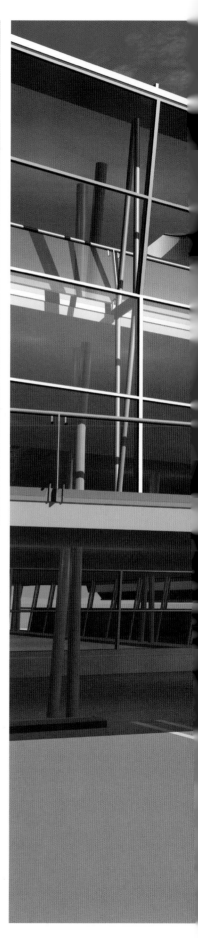

View of western curtain wall

Corrugated Duct House

Project No. 9804
Palm Springs, California
1998

The desert mountain ranges in the Coachella Valley and the dramatic heat and sunshine of Palm Springs, California, form the context for this experimental house. Its concept is derived from the position that because air conditioning is unavoidable in this area, then environmental microconditions, as expressed in spatial and material conditions, can drive the organization and techniques of construction and HVAC. Preliminary research was done as follows:

Research I
— *Golf course architects: Geometry and contours, grass types, watering systems.*
— *Cultural research on suburban landscape techniques that produce the "molded landscape"—cacti, white gravel, hedge geometry, etc.*
— *Swimming pools: Shapes in plan and section, chlorinating systems, diving boards.*
— *All types of artificial gardens, landscapes (Zen Gardens like Ryo-anji), etc. The work of Roberto Burle-Marx.*
— *Vertical nature systems like ivy.*

Research II
— *Building systems and structural details. Emphasis on envelope types and environmental control aspects—for example, louvers and solar shading devices, mullion/glazing systems, both structural and lightweight (intelligent facades).*
— *Concrete foundation techniques.*
— *Wood and steel superstructure framing systems.*
— *Building materials: Translucent and opaque panels or sheets (wood, plastic, aluminum). "Soft" skins of fabric or molded surfaces.*
— *Ergonomic aspects of furniture, freestanding and built in.*
— *Industrial products: Automobiles (styling and interiors). Lawnmowers, televisions, refrigerators, vacuum cleaners, etc.*

Research III
— *Tree types, both indigenous and cultivated for Southern California climate.*
— *Natural and artificial plant material for the region.*
— *Existing landscape geometries and surface conditions (flat and three-dimensional grids).*
— *Historical research into the desert and its geological formation.*
— *Solar data: Temperatures (dry bulb, wet bulb), heating degree days, micro-climates relative to elevation.*
— *Water: Reservoirs, storage, hydraulic speed (flows). How water works in wetlands, fisheries, etc.*

Research IV
— *Heating, ventilation, and air-conditioning systems (HVAC). Residential and small-scale industrial and commercial buildings. Convection, forced air, etc. Ducts, chases, plenums. Air-handling units: centralized, rooftop. Fresh air intake systems. Vents and grilles.*
— *Product information, images of systems, dimensions, company logos, etc.*
— *Lighting and electrical: Quartz, halogen, halide, fluorescent, etc., mostly for exterior use.*

Programmatically, the house is 2,000 square feet of conditioned space with a flexible interior. Two bedrooms and 1.5 baths are required for private spaces, while the kitchen and living spaces merge in and between the structure/plenum system. Parking for two cars fits below the roof.

The scheme is oriented around a large, white-painted corrugated steel roof. Constructed from 1/8-inch steel sheet, the roof section is a series of supersized corrugations mirrored top and bottom to form structural depth and HVAC plenums. The double-skin cavity roof system reflects heat so that cool air and water can flow through the plenums to the interior of the house. Air-handling units are attached to the roof edges.

While the corrugations mainly form the roof, they also twist and turn to form random columns/chases/shafts as well as exterior wall fragments, internal partitions, and built-in furniture. Cool air flows through the entire system, with small vents and registers placed in precise ways to cool the body inside the house. Micro-environments are formed also through humidity control and misting systems. A terrazzo floor and aluminum and glass curtain walls complete the material conditions of the house.

Detail of south side HVAC roof system

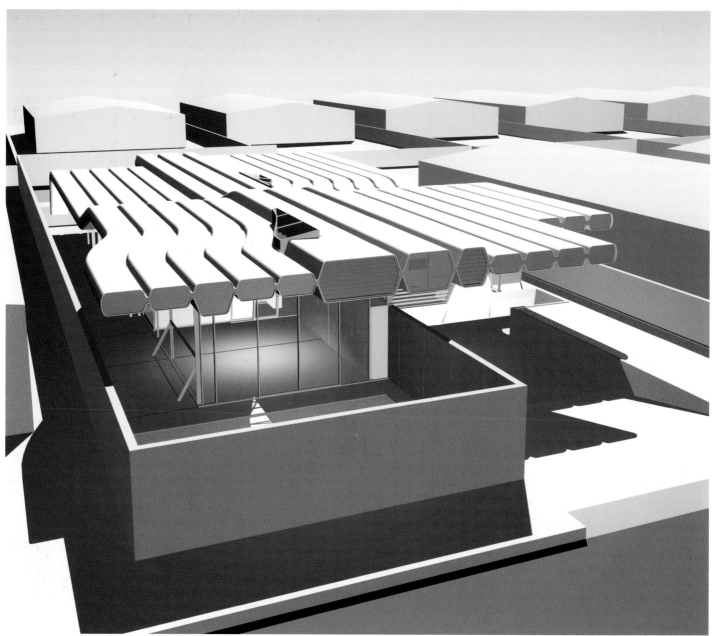

Aerial view from the north

View from the street

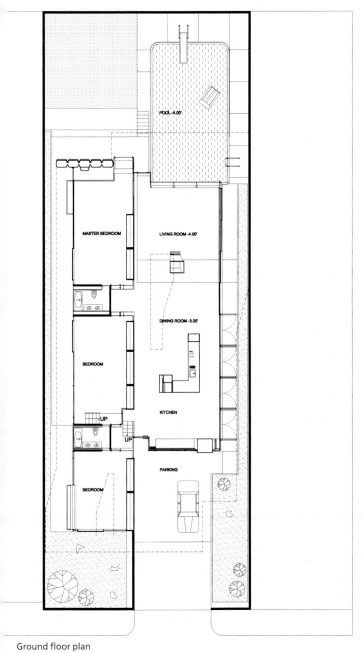

Ground floor plan

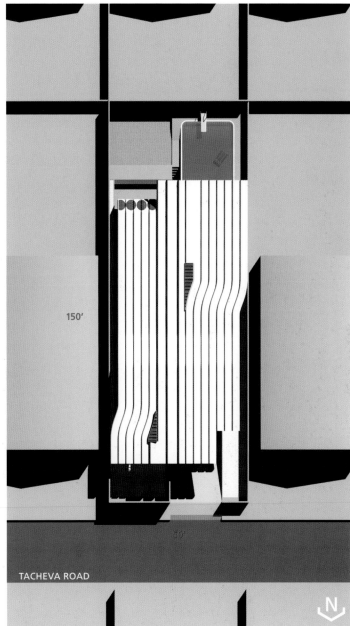

Site plan

TACHEVA ROAD

150'

50'

N

View of front entrance

View into bedroom 2

Interior looking toward front door

Views of public zones

View of rear yard from across lawn

View across pool into house

View across pool into house

Project No. 9706
San Francisco, California
1997–1998

Why?

In a world where marketplace domination by a single company may be seen as either the zenith of laissez-faire capitalism or, contrarily, as the suffocation of competition, Microsoft moves in and out of both conditions, gaining market share through scale and product marketing. At the end of the twentieth century, with computers and software still a new frontier in the realm of mass culture, Microsoft decided to ask two important questions about the company and, indeed, about architecture.

Question 1 may be stated like this: *Because we only sell code, zeroes and ones, because our operating system is preloaded on 95 percent of all computers in the world, and because new software, upgrades, and so on may be purchased online and at national computer chain stores, why should we propose to have a retail store for our products? Why the need to spatialize a product when, beyond its packaging, it is essentially immaterial?*

If question 1 may in fact be answered with the idea that market presence must now include real spaces in addition to the virtual fields of sales, then question 2 must be: *What will Microsoft look and feel like as a company when materialized through the spatial medium of architecture? Because the corporate campus at Redmond, Washington, is simply a well-designed, functional home to the company, not an advertising symbol,and with no other permanent architectural installation anywhere else, won't Microsoft need a new discourse on identity?*

Identity

The clients asked for a concept design for the first Microsoft retail store, to be located in a 10,000-square-foot interior in the SONY Metreon building currently under construction on the Yerba Buena plateau in San Francisco. Named Microsoft.SF (with Tokyo and Berlin to follow), the scheme was generated in collaboration with Wieden + Kennedy Advertising Agency of Portland (Whitney Lowe, lead graphic designer), SONY Development of Burbank (Richard Altuna, retail consultant), and Microsoft western regional sales management. The client wishes to enter the retail market through a real architectural presence. This project attempts to deliver, in architectural terms, the aura of digital technology as well as the purposeful tools that Microsoft has developed for working, living, and learning.

The store is located between two attraction stores: a Mœbius-designed video arcade and a David Macauley "The Way Things Work" landscape. As a result, the Microsoft store demands that a pathway be created to move through the space. Unlike a typical shopping mall, where the "street" is lined with stores, the SONY Metreon opts for an *en filade* arrangement of spaces with no circulation space outside of a store.

Media Pathway

In our final scheme, the resultant pathway curves deeply into the space of the store, lined with electron-reversing glass skins. By employing Viracon® glass, which with the flip of a switch can become a white, opaque surface, these two skins allow what is otherwise problematic for store design: walls. But as these walls temporarily block views across the store, projectors located in the smoothly molded ceiling system send text, ad tag lines, and special film clips onto the glass, creating a media path. The pathway opens up in the heart of the store to 30 feet wide to create a moment where the path mutates into placeform. Inserted into the glass panels are interactive seats where visitors may engage with new software, surf the Web, or watch MSNBC. Beyond the glass skins are fields of software presented in special display structures loaded with flatscreen technology.

View from interior back to entrance (view 3)
From the first scheme

First Scheme

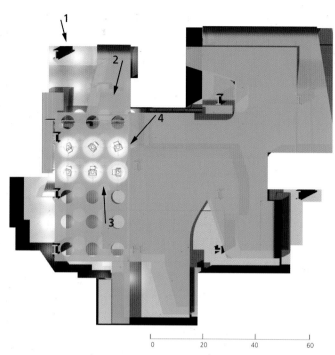

First scheme floor plan, with numbers indicating view angles

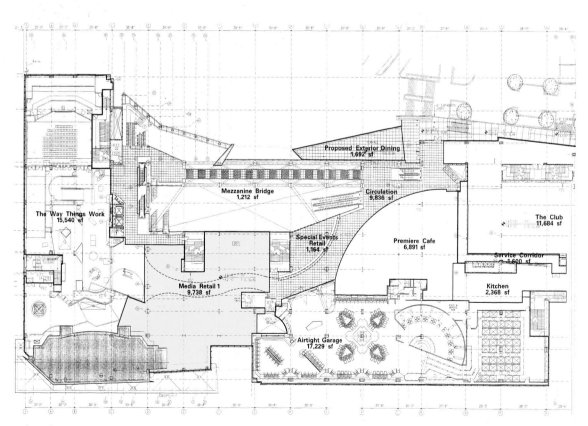

Floor plan, SONY Metreon Complex

View of entrance

First Scheme

View from cashier's station

4

View across suspended-computer landscape

Final Scheme

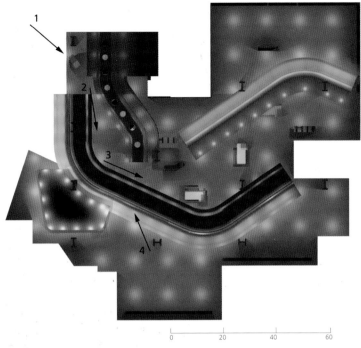

Floor plan, second scheme, with numbers indicating view angles

Views through media pathway

Views through media pathway

Project No. 9605
Arlington, Texas
1996

The Hegemony of Amusement

Arlington, Texas, is the 58th largest city in the United States, with a population of nearly 300,000 people. It lies six miles south of the Dallas–Fort Worth International Airport and is roughly on a center line between those two cities, themselves 34 miles apart. As part of the Dallas–Fort Worth Metroplex, Arlington has more than tripled in size since 1970. With the original Six Flags amusement park, the 1972 entrance of a major-league baseball franchise, and still newer hyperaquatic parks, Arlington has defined itself as a large-scale outdoor entertainment center of national renown. Though City Hall and the Central Library are some four miles to the west of this major agglomeration of family fun, it is widely acknowledged, even by the politicians, that the center of activity of the city is now constituted by these entertainment systems.

Since 1990, the Arlington Museum of Art has been located in a white, modernist brick box built originally in 1957 as a J.C. Penney department store. It was renovated to its present state in 1992. Privately funded, it resides in the city in two conspicuously ambivalent ways. First, it sits on Main Street in the original town center, a now sparsely populated zone with tentative commercial viability. Its precise position is just to the north of city hall, a 1970s brick building with council chambers rotated at 45 degrees. This common formal move of the day precipitated the deflection of Main Street from its east-west orientation, creating a triangular open space contiguous to the east side of the museum, a space to be developed as a public park. With no party-wall building to the east, the symmetry of the museum exists in sharp contrast to the oblique emptiness of the site conditions. Here, one asks if the museum is at the beginning or the end of Main Street.

The second ambivalence of the museum is that although it is not publicly funded, it is adjacent to two public buildings: City Hall and the central library. The public therefore is not sure if the museum is integral to public life or if it is a detached vessel of alienating artistic pretensions.

Modernist Expediency

Critics of modern architecture have quite often described it as a nearly century-long project to wage war on the outmoded or conventional forms of expression that once had their time but through cultural inertia or fear persist in mainstream production. In 1957, in Arlington, the modern was simply a space of neutrality where abstraction was an expedient style, not a cultural belief. J.C. Penney, therefore, arrived as a volume of pure space with racks of affordable clothes made of new synthetic materials for the postwar space-race family.

So, with abstract geometry and whiteness as both its great neutralizer and its signifier of modernism, the Arlington Museum of Art is now an even more appropriate function for the space and for the city. In fact, since 1992, the direction of the museum has explicitly restated the convivial and, indeed, more connected aspects of modern art through educational programs and public events with the art as a backdrop.

Continuity/Difference

The client, an energetic, forward-thinking director and curator, asked that the building be simultaneously transformed and preserved. In a city full of decorative commercial architecture (no different than most of North America), the museum has generated its own iconography through minimal appearances, suggesting that an upstaging of this evanescent quality would subtract from the *gestalt* already there. The brief called for a renovation of the existing building and for two other components that would occupy public land: a small park and an addition of some 3,000 square feet. These two aspects of the program were to be presented and arbitrated, but not paid for, by the city of Arlington.

The existing building consists of 20,000 square feet, with street-level and basement floors of 8,650 square feet each and a mezzanine of 3,250 square feet. The perimeter walls are load-bearing masonry with a 25-foot bay steel structural grid. The basement, now a dark space used for storage, is to have a new exhibition/performance space, two teaching spaces with material storage, and a shop for exhibit preparation and storage. The main floor will include an entrance hall, double-height exhibition spaces, and a new café. The mezzanine will contain offices, library, and exhibition space for small works.

The sequence of events whereby the design evolved:

1. Preserve the emptiness and whiteness of the building and, in particular, the upper section of the front facade. The embossed grid is assessed as a graphic reiteration of the right angle and of neutralization, akin to the pure material expressions of the paintings of Robert Ryman.

2. Remove all existing storefront and begin to restate the transparency of glass while controlling the hot sun on a south-facing orientation. This is done by sloping the glass toward the interior. A 16-foot portion of the glass curtain wall slides horizontally. This allows the loading of large objects, which becomes a spectacle on Main Street when large works arrive for an exhibition.

3. Rid the building of its symmetry by moving the entry to the west end of the front facade. After all, because there is no building on the east side of the museum, it is not symmetrical in the city context. This position sets up a new process to enter the building—a controlled prelude to the open and free space of the center of the museum. By acknowledging the corners of the building, oblique angles of experience are set up that move the visitor farther away from the existing symmetry.

4. Place an 8-foot-high wall parallel to and 16 feet behind the new glass curtain wall. This creates an entrance hall that is filled with light but intended to protect the gallery spaces inside.

5. Insert an elevator diagonally opposite the point where the visitor emerges from the entrance hall to the exhibition space. This machine connects the basement floor to the roof deck, allowing every horizontal surface to be used. The steel structure of the elevator shaft is skinned with translucent polycarbonate sheets.

6. Lower the ground in the public park 5 feet to let light into an otherwise dark basement level with clerestory windows. The space made in the park will allow the café to extend outside into the green space and will socially connect the museum to the city.

7. Ask the question: Is it possible to build an addition that would not only produce more space for the museum but also define an institutional quality that seems, at present, to be an idea more than an architecture? And to do it in the space of an open, public park in a city that is yet to fully embrace urbanism?

8. Answer the above question by projecting an addition built on steel columns that continues the curving edge of Main Street and also resolves the end of Pecan Street as a north-south corridor. The metal-clad wing is a simple volumetric object that extracts its dimensions from the existing building. The pattern of the metal seams is intended to continue the surface treatment of the existing building (the embossed grid) without replicating it.

Main Street facade

ARLINGTON MUSEUM OF ART

Pecan Street view of existing building

Pecan Street view of addition

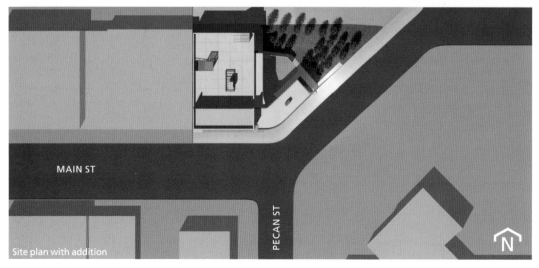

Site plan with addition

MAIN ST

PECAN ST

N

Night view of addition

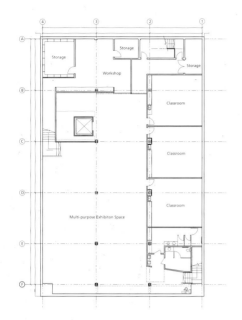

Basement level plan

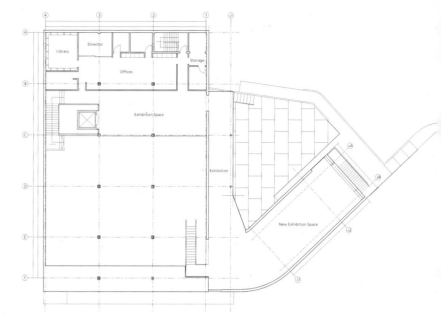

Mezzanine level plan

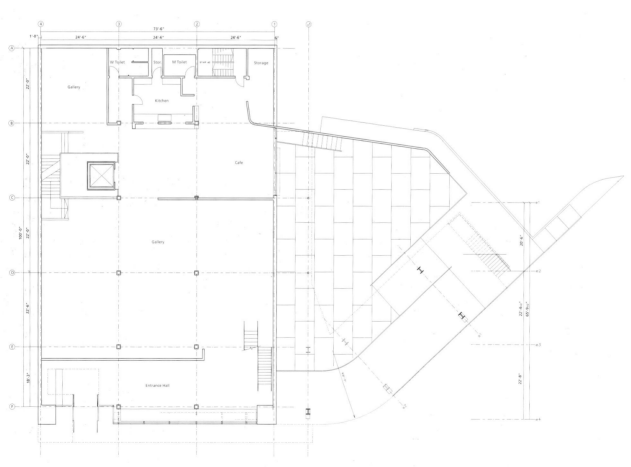

Ground level plan

Northeast aerial view

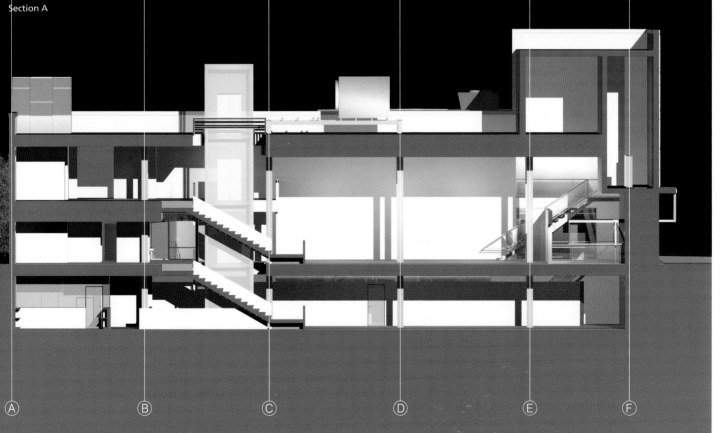

Section A

Ⓐ   Ⓑ   Ⓒ   Ⓓ   Ⓔ   Ⓕ

View under addition

View of main exhibition space

Interior view of entrance

View of stairs to addition

Entrance hall

Sliding curtain wall

Project No. 9304
New York, New York
1993

Manhattan: Specific/Grid: Not

Originally commissioned in 1990 by a new subdivision of Steelcase, the large manu-facturer of office furniture, this project is the result of five schemes developed over a three-year period. The company, named Details, asked for a "wall" that would divide a 2,000-square-foot loft space in SoHo, New York, into two distinct spaces, each of which would have a different but related function. One space is defined as clerical (order entry), the other as a design studio. The function of the wall, beyond its own properties of bisection, is storage for books and prototypes; one end houses a worktable underneath the fiberglass skin. The basic position of the wall in the space was given by the client.

The project operates as an information cipher that passes through the space, becoming reified in form within the room itself. The room, however, is considered to be insignificant and serves only to cut the information vapor that is conceptu-ally moving through the entire Euclidean matrix of Manhattan. The wall, there-fore, is not site driven and accommodates entry by making functional cuts into the white skin.

Molds and Plasmas

Sectionally, the molded surface changes constantly along its length, accommo-dating the shifts in program, generating a kind of regional ergonomic specificity. One asks here if it is possible to shrink-wrap program. As this project is scaled to the body, not unlike an automobile, human factors become the metrical limits to the form. Each section is made up of multiple arcs, all joined at a point of oscula-tion. Diagrammatically, each center that generates an arc is understood to be a point of significance that conspires with other centers in the sectional shape to define a bundle of pathways. These pathways, formed by centers and periph-eries, are symbolic of the currents of which cities are made: markets, politics, technologies, etc.

Structurally, the molded skin supports itself, as it is sectionally curving or loosely corrugated, resulting in a higher degree of dynamic stiffness. It is made in 110-centimeter-wide sections of fiberglass panels bolted together. It sits on top of a welded and bolted aluminum structural tube frame that supports the floor and table.

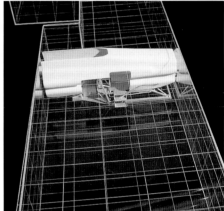

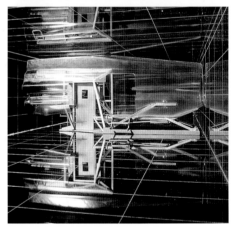

Final scheme

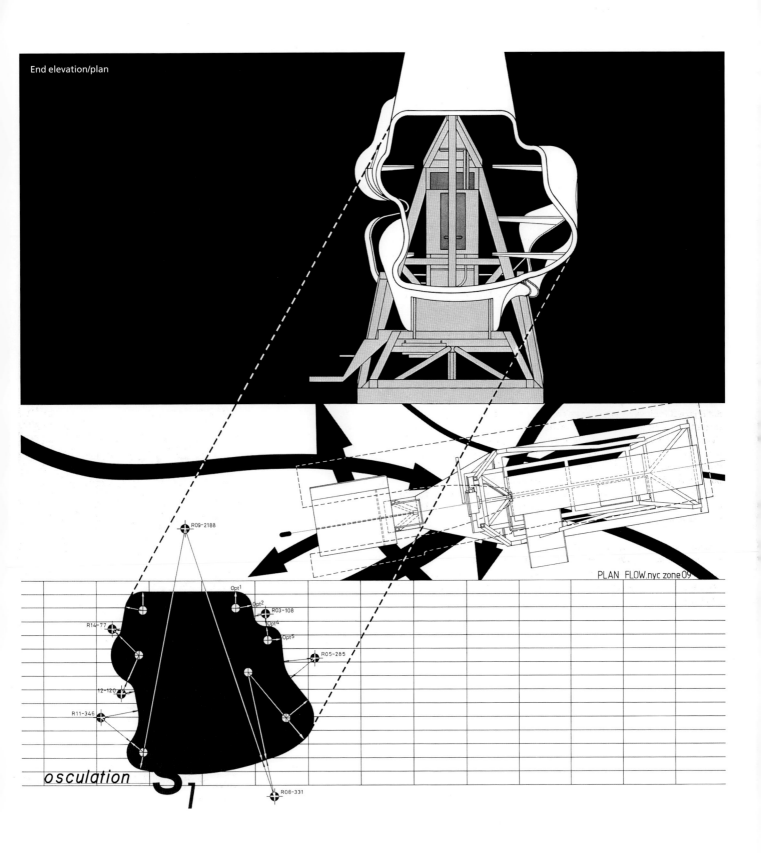

End elevation/plan

PLAN FLOW.nyc zone 09

R09-2188

Opt¹

Opt²

R03-108

R14-77

Opt⁴

Opt⁵

R05-285

12-120

R11-346

osculation

R08-331

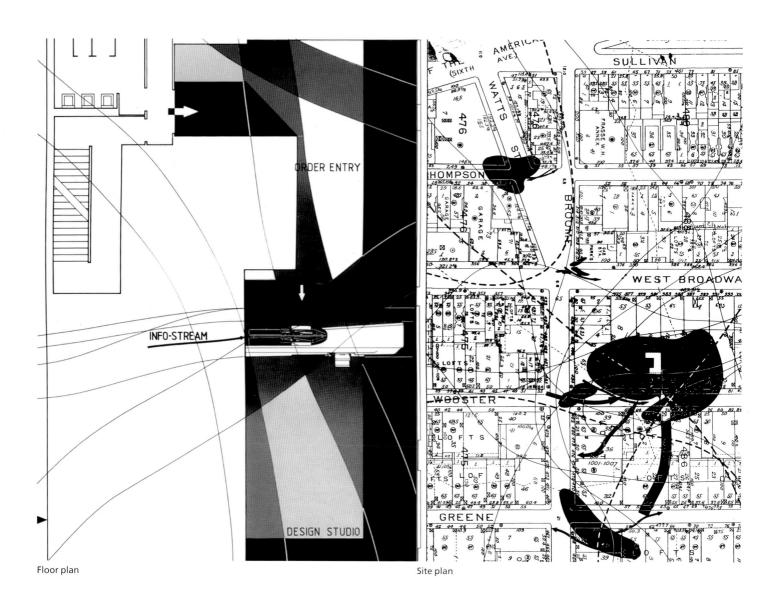

ORDER ENTRY

INFO-STREAM

DESIGN STUDIO

Floor plan

Site plan

Side elevations

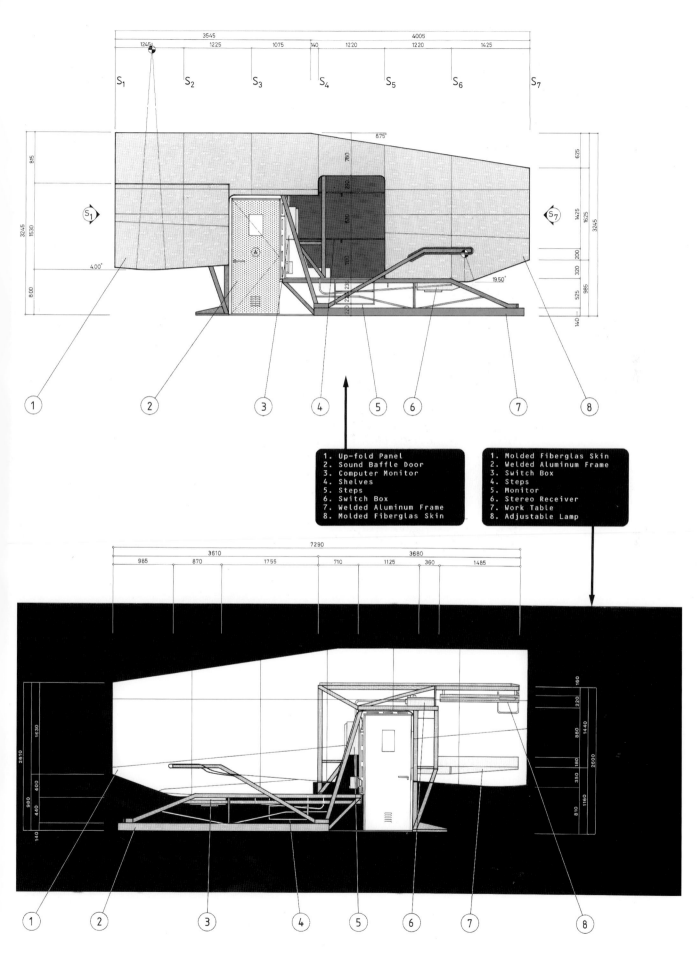

1. Up-fold Panel
2. Sound Baffle Door
3. Computer Monitor
4. Shelves
5. Steps
6. Switch Box
7. Welded Aluminum Frame
8. Molded Fiberglas Skin

1. Molded Fiberglas Skin
2. Welded Aluminum Frame
3. Switch Box
4. Steps
5. Monitor
6. Stereo Receiver
7. Work Table
8. Adjustable Lamp

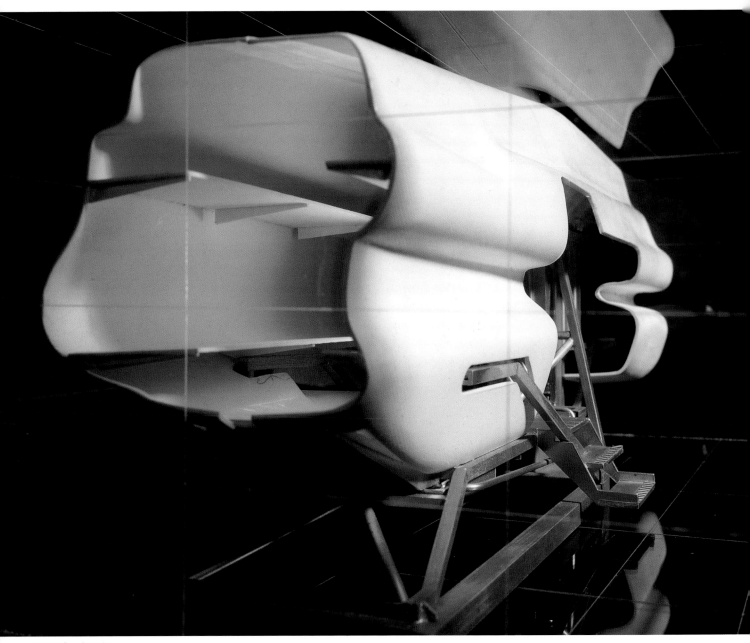

View of end section

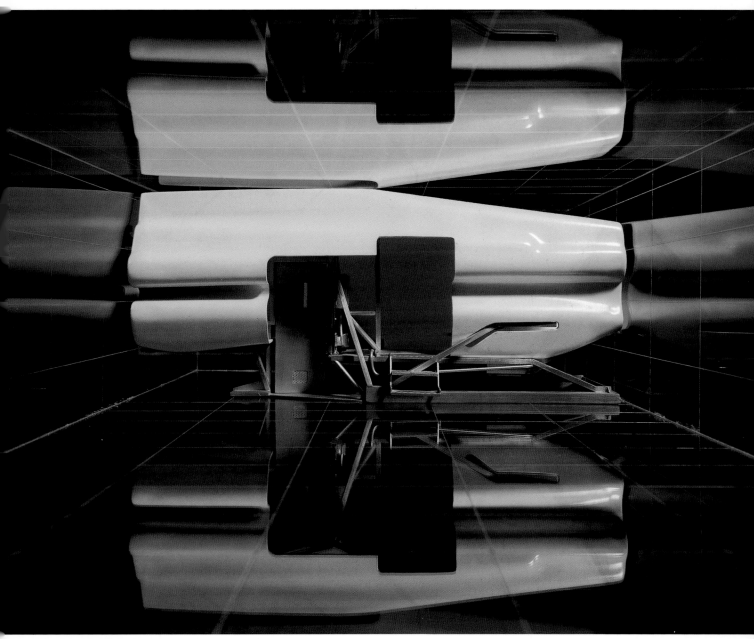

View from design studio

Project No. 9601
Tokyo, Japan
1996

Sited just above the Nogizaka Subway Station and adjacent to Roppongi in Tokyo, Gallery MA is a fourteen-year-old space devoted to exhibiting architecture and related design. This project was inserted into the third floor of a six-floor building. On this level, an external quasi–Zen garden bounded by concrete walls cuts the floors above in half, creating a L-shaped building mass. A glass membrane divides the interior space from the garden and allows total visual invasion of the inserted project. The space is approximately 6.5 x 11 meters in plan and 2.45 meters in section.

The program for the project was an experimental space.

The design scheme for Gallery MA is developed from the Homolosine Interrupted Projection Mapping System. The origin of the word *map* is in a word meaning sheet, merely a surface to record territories on. The Homolosine Projection depicts the world in a series of sheared ellipses — thus the green surface inside Gallery MA is an interrupted projection, as it deploys a flattened and empty global surface to form space. The surface bends and loops to form a three-dimensionally smooth yet complex geometry capable of merging with the graphically logoized world of visual codes and conventional signs. This is the worldsheet.

Logos of fictional companies such as Overcodes and Univocal are printed on the worldsheet. Each logo has a bar code next to it that triggers information onto a hand-held camera/screen known as a Navicam, a device in development by Sony.

The detailed design argument is as follows:

I
The system or matrix of objects constitutes the material production of the world.
In theory, objects have a use value or an instrumental nature. They are developed from existing or potential needs and desires of culture. Despite the utilitarian value of most objects, the possibility exists for any object to signify a status of itself or its user. Exchange value of an object is determined in the market system of all related objects. Here, the object is a commodity. What follows from this is the symbolic or signform value of the object where performance, need, or utility fall away in the face of another, more superficial iconography of value, such as the image or the logo.

II
Mass-produced consumer objects are deployed, producing corporate wealth and identity.
The corporation, upon inspection, has perhaps the greatest degree of indifference to cultural or physiological needs in determining the possible production of an object. The logic of capitalism is primarily a kind of cultural logic. Product and company identity, usually manifest through advertising and graphic design, operate as a type of saturated code — that is, where the logo appears over and over again in all corners of the world.

III
The signform overtakes/occludes the object as referent. The stretchy, logoized fabric is invented: worldsheet.
The logo or identifying symbol becomes a sign or, further, a code in the move from an object-based to a graphic-based culture. Like DNA and computer codes, the graphic sign codes may be mapped and programmed to carry out certain tasks or performances. In the case of the graphic, the task may be that of seduction or of infinite reproduction. It is possible, then , to imagine how the fluid plasmas of economics, communications, entertainment, and so on collapse onto a single homogeneous worldskin.

The code for printing is the CMYK strip. The code for video projection is the trio of RGB lenses. They conspire to make the images readable.

IV
This produces another global surface of practically homogeneous signforms.
Through technology, the concept of the local site or real ground is changed. Digital technology is especially indifferent to location (electricity can be everywhere a battery can go!). The world, in terms of technology, is more like a map than a real sphere. Perhaps it could even be called a graph, where information such as gross national product (GNP) is more important than how many square miles of land a country or city has.

V
Map *comes from the Latin word for sheet. Its origins are not in information but in the geometry of the flat surface.*
As a two-dimensional plane, the sheet must be bent in order to architecturally spatialize a phenomenon. Its flatness is overcome by the powerful ability for architecture to momentarily intensify the graphic surface of seduction.

VI
Goode's Interrupted Homolosine Projection depicts the world in a two-dimensional series of sheared ellipses.
This projection system is a combination of the Sinusoidal and Mollweide grids. The grids are interrupted and combined so that land masses can be projected with a minimum of shape distortion by positioning each section on a separate central meridian.

VII
Erase geographic information on the interrupted projection.
We are left with a *silhouette du mondial* (outline of the world). Fill in with logos and text for a realigned world. Projections of all kinds proliferate, crisscrossing and interrupting, flowing on and canceling out.

View of installation

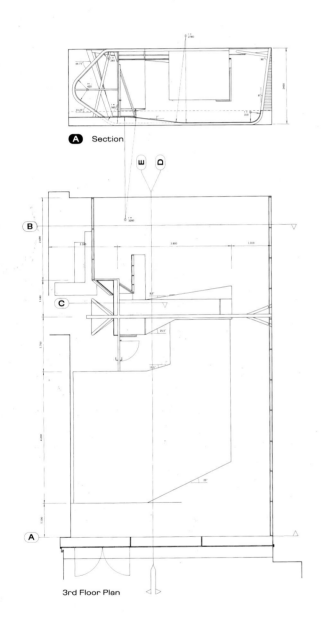

A Section

B Section

C Partial Section

D Section

E Section

F Partial Plan

3rd Floor Plan

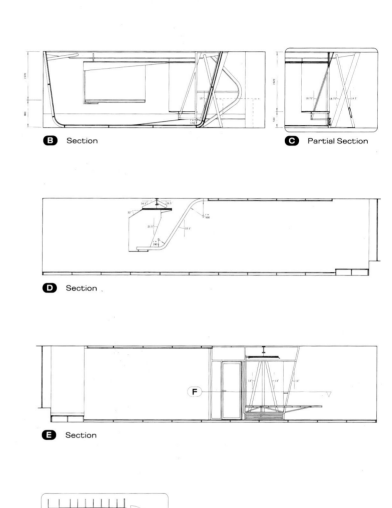

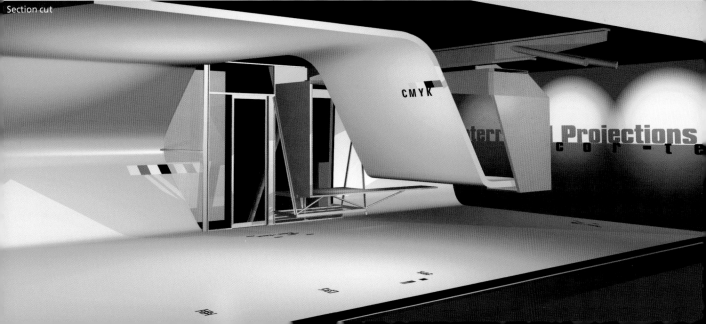

Views of installation

163

Project No. 9303
Tokyo, Japan
1992–1993

Dense Yet Free

In the programmatic form of a three-bedroom, two-bath house, this project is deployed into the Tokyo matrix as a prototype house that reaches the typical density of that city's land value economy while pushing into a spatial complexity of movement and flexibility. The client, a private developer, wanted to study the possibilities of such a condition.

The site is a rectangle of 14 x 7 meters, which is typical for the outer wards of Tokyo such as Setagaya and Shinagawa. The scheme inverts the usual privatization often seen in Tokyo as opaque walls containing inward-focused rooms (Tadao Ando, for instance). It does so by dematerializing the sides with an array of glazed and molded skins intended to be more expressive of the interior. Meanwhile, the roof-form serves as an arcing datum line for the house. The bedrooms, encoded by the blue walls, spiral up into the space and penetrate the roof to describe the z-axis or vertical limits to the site.

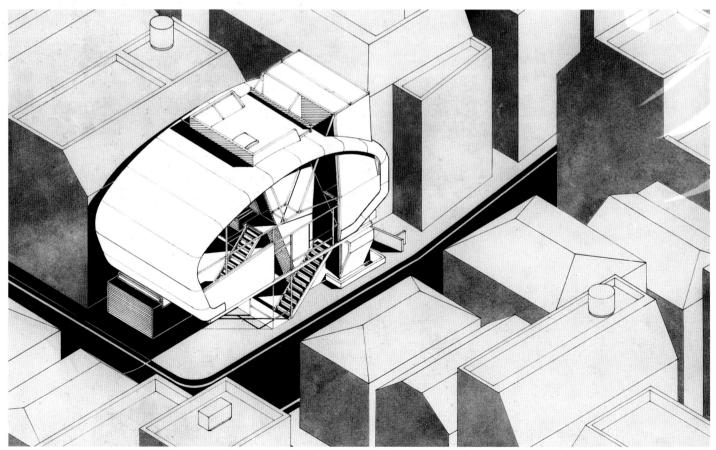

Axonometric City view

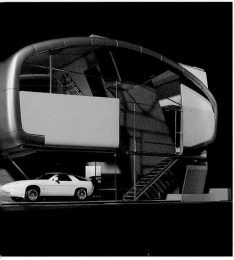
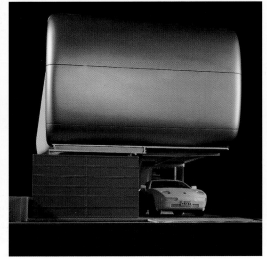

Views

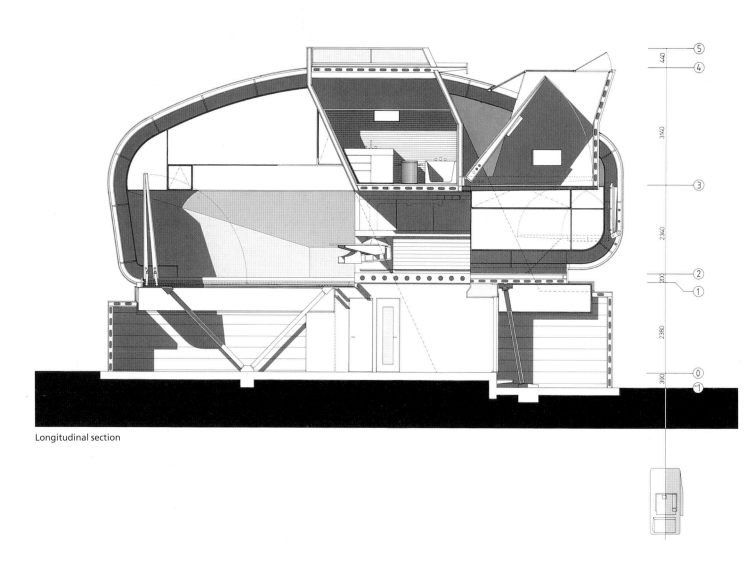

Longitudinal section

Cross sections

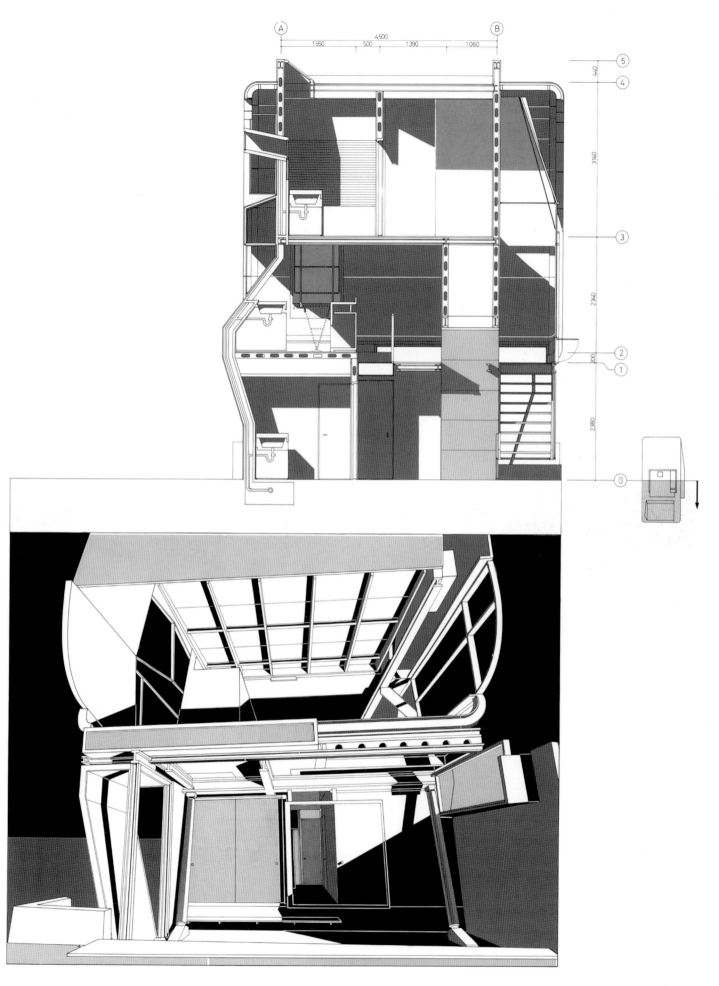

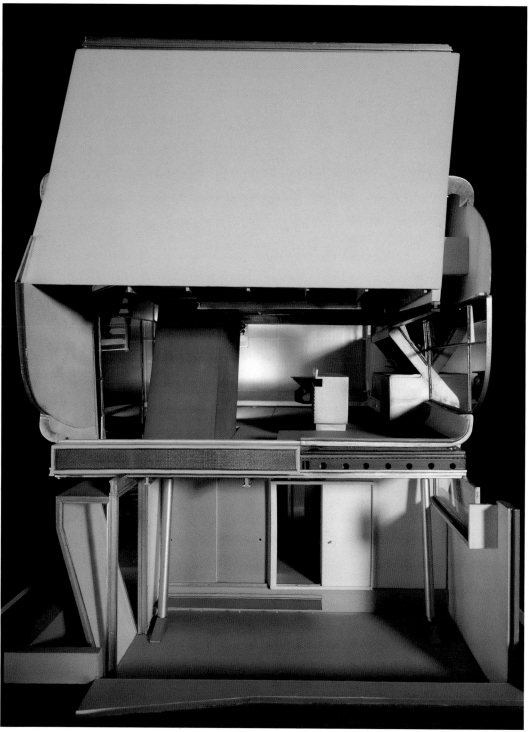

Sectional model

Detail views

Tokyo Minimum High-Rise Housing (Vertical Weekly Mansion)

Project No. 9501
Tokyo, Japan
1995

Unbelievable Rents

The weekly mansion is an existing type of temporary housing in Tokyo. Normally structured as multistory single-loaded corridor slab buildings, these projects maximize land value by charging extremely high monthly rents for the fluctuating residencies of itinerant salarymen and women. The convenience of this type of housing, usually located within the center of Tokyo or its immediate periphery, allows companies or universities (for instance) to mobilize their workforce quite easily.

As Tokyo land area must be vertically expanded and economically densified, the 30-meter-high Vertical Weekly Mansion (*mansion* being one of the more humorous oxymoronic loan words in Japanese, as these units are less than 25 square meters in size, yet the rents can be as high as $2,000 per month) is a building projected for a 68.675-square-meter (6.7 meters x 10.25 meters) site footprint in the Aoyama sector of Tokyo, home to many corporate headquarters, including C-ITOH and Honda. Seven repetitive floors of one-room apartments are stacked between an entrance space on the ground level and a two-level multipurpose bar and meeting space at the top of the high-rise. In the basement level, space is divided between a public bar in front and the service areas (laundry and trash compaction) in the back.

Efficiency + Minor Dysfunction

Largely functionally determined, this project is indeed straightforward architecture. The zoning envelope in Tokyo allows a vertical extrusion up to 30 meters; above that the building mass must slope back by 45 degrees. With the site so small, in this case, there is no room to slope back above the site perimeter. Floor area ratios, budgets, structure (strict earthquake codes), and so on all seem to determine the conventional building in Tokyo. The high-rise prototype asserts difference by treating the interior apartment as an industrial design where aluminum tables and soft futons are concealed in the floor surface for temporary pop-up use. Each apartment contains video projection and flatscreen LCD wall panels.

The structure features a reinforced-concrete service core acting as the main column, with concrete floors and bracing for the units. Steel stairs are cantilevered from the rear side of the concrete core. Electron-inverting glass and aluminum panels are the main external cladding materials.

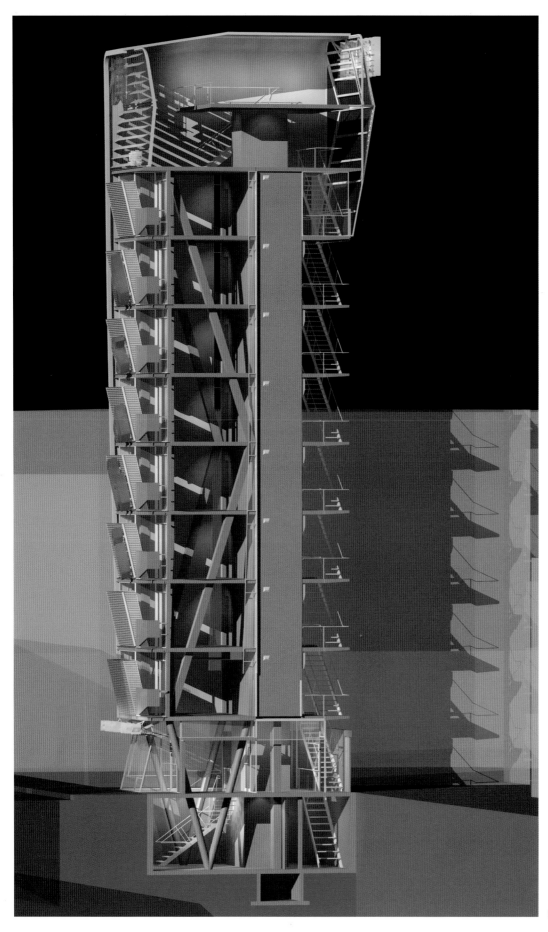

Section

Rear elevation

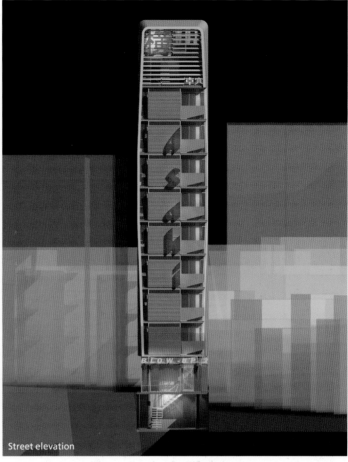

Street elevation

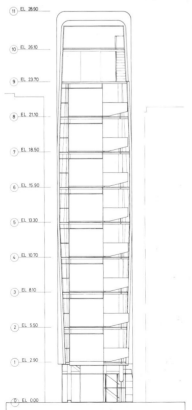

Front elevation

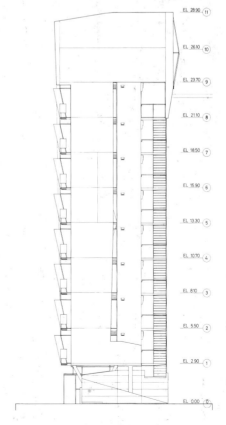

Typical side elevation

175

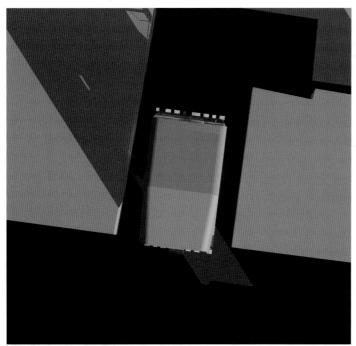

Site plan: Shibuya

Aerial view

Detail of top signage

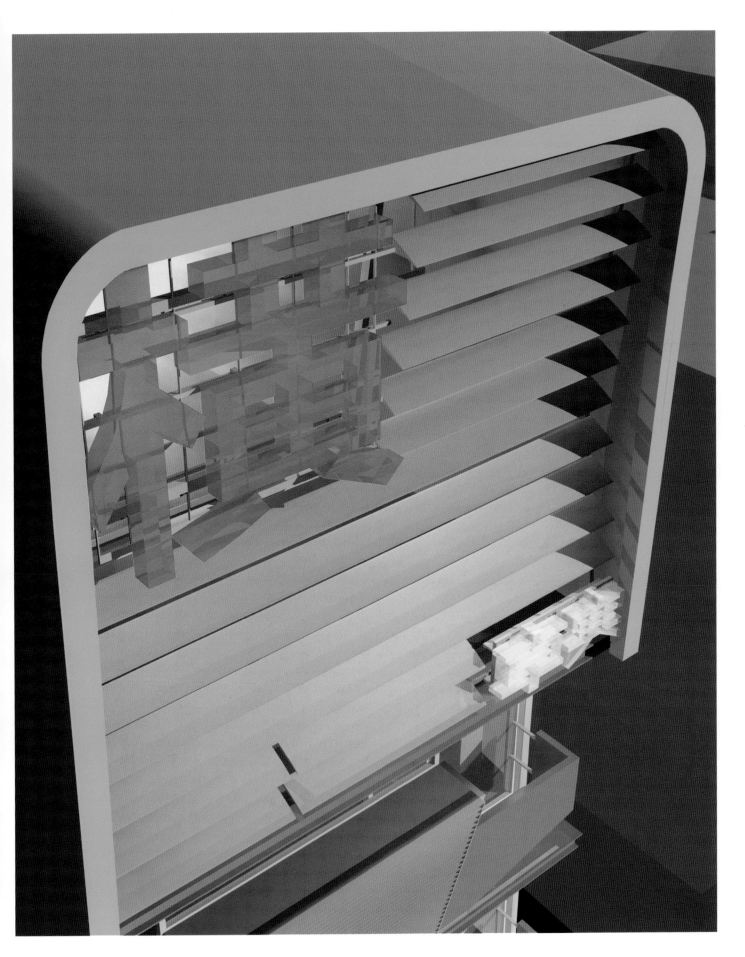

Exploded view of building component

Floor plans

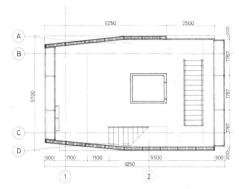

FREE SPACE LEVEL   EL 23.700

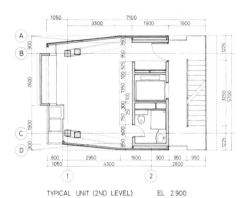

TYPICAL UNIT (2ND LEVEL)   EL 2.900

ENTRANCE / STREET LEVEL   EL 0.000

SERVICE / BAR LEVEL   EL -2.900

View at top rear

Detail view of rear

View up the front

Street view

Detail of entrance lobby

Sectional detail of basement

Aerial view of twin version

Section of twin version

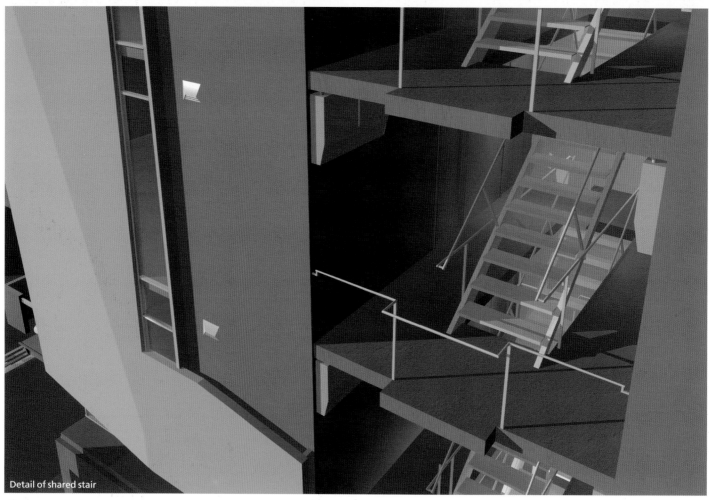
Detail of shared stair

View up twin version

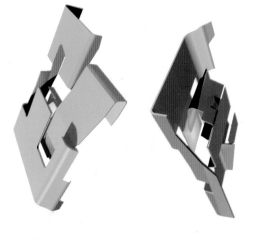

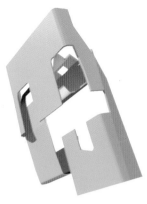

Worldsheets

Kansai-kan Library Competition

Project No. 9602
Kansai Science City, Japan
1996

Books.com

At the end of the twentieth century, the program of the library and its relation to architecture has mutated into an open-ended problem sponsored by the rise in digital communications systems. Traditional aspects of libraries, such as centrality, accessibility, and, indeed, physicality, are called into question as more and more information and research is conducted outside the vessel of public architecture, facilitated by the advent of megabookstores, on-line bookstores, and the Web in general. An outcome of this is the commercialization of knowledge, which has been folded into a consumer discourse where the social condition of learning takes place in malls and bookstores instead of in the main reading rooms of most libraries. Nonetheless, even as home libraries become more effective because of consumer accessibility to contemporary information, libraries for cities and entire countries are being built as historical repositories, if for no other reason.

Corporate Funding

Sited in the Keihanna Hills between Kyoto, Nara, and Osaka, a densely populated cultural region known as the Kansai area, the National Library is accessible to millions of people living less than thirty minutes away by train. Specifically, the project is to be built in the new technopolis of Kansai Science City, population 380,000, where corporate research and development installations, sprawling office parks, hotels, and fabricated zones of park space are located. Set against the lush hills, this is a technoscientific oasis of vast artificiality. It is set up as a series of twelve nodes rather than in a centralized pattern.

The private-sector initiative in the construction of Kansai Science City, including interests from Sumitomo, Matsushita, and Kawasaki Steel, provided financial support to a project that could never have been sustained by government funding alone. In 1987, the National Diet confirmed that the central library of Japan would be located there as a massive resource for the technology-based culture around it.

On a site of 37,500 square meters, the building coverage is to be less than 70 percent of the entire block. The total program of 60,000 square meters is evenly divided among the stacks department and all other functions. Two large reading rooms, one general, the other for Asian studies, dominate the support program, which also includes administration, operational systems, public auditoriums and seminar rooms, and so on.

Very Big Worldsheets

In contrast to the diminishing aspect of public space, rendered especially clear in the suburban layout of the Science City, the scheme reasserts the power of architectural space. It does so via two conditions. One, given that the site allows distant views across it, a building of expressive potential was possible. Therefore, the temptations to make the building disappear (underground) or become urbanized (as a wall to the street) were not explored. Two, given that the program is not intended to be a large, open lending institution, insisting on making the building a diagram of certain forms of contemporary knowledge was the only option as a reaction to this implicit privatization.

The scheme breaks down into three parts that function as both discrete and integrated elements. The entire stack program is located within a concrete box on the southern edge of the site. As the site slopes up from north to south, the stack building is largely submerged into the ground. Across a service road to the north of this element, a large parking surface is covered by a public park and plaza. Sitting on top of but not disengaged from these two elements, the superstructure of the building asserts public space through its surface connection to the exterior. This building consists of two superscaled worldsheets that interact to form continuous surfaces that intersect with the matrix of floor plates and columnar systems of the structure.

The program for the Kansai-kan National Diet Library of Japan reflects this condition. Proposed for a country of unusually high literacy, this building will house all of the future production of printed and digital knowledge at one location. Intended more for on-site research than community lending, the inflection of the program toward a private corporate and scientific elite supports, at one level, the demise of the public library and, at another, points to the shift from a material to a digital culture.

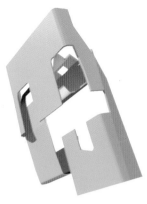

site

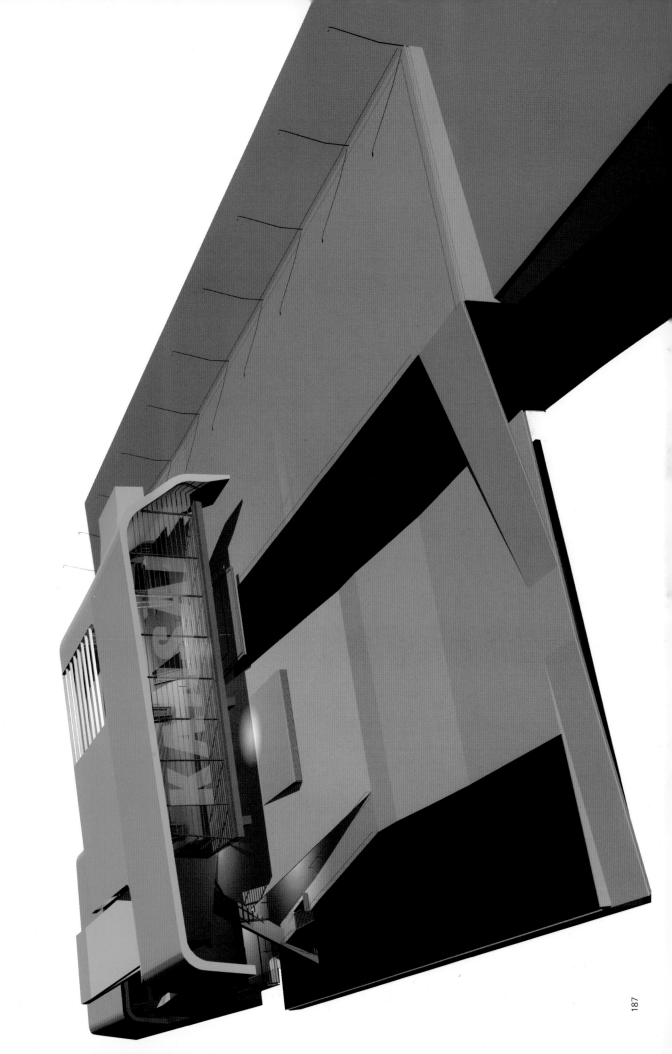

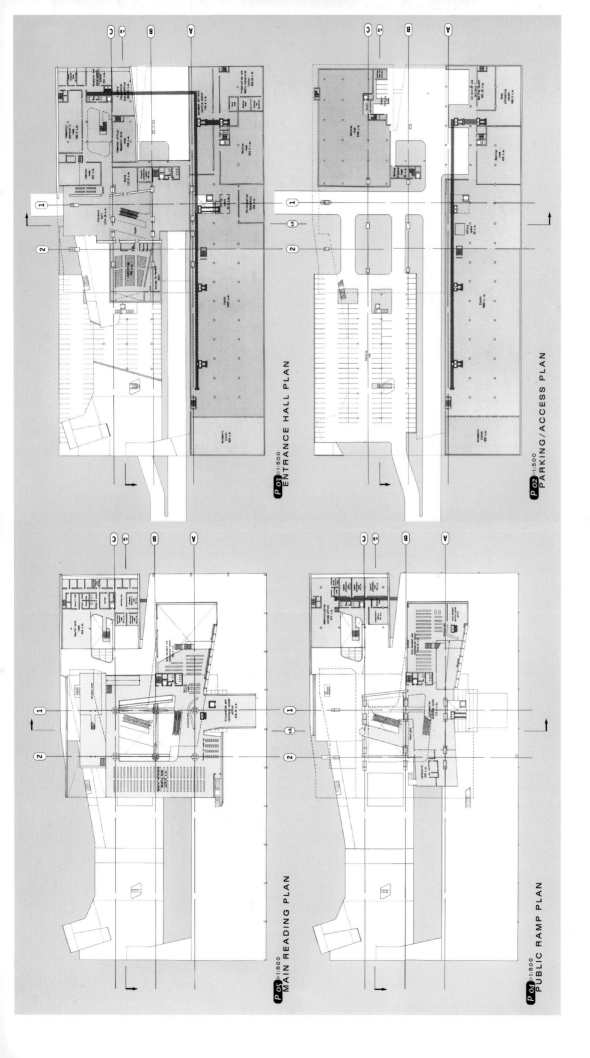

P 03 ▷ 1:500
ENTRANCE HALL PLAN

P 02 ▷ 1:500
PARKING/ACCESS PLAN

P 05 ▷ 1:500
MAIN READING PLAN

P 04 ▷ 1:500
PUBLIC RAMP PLAN

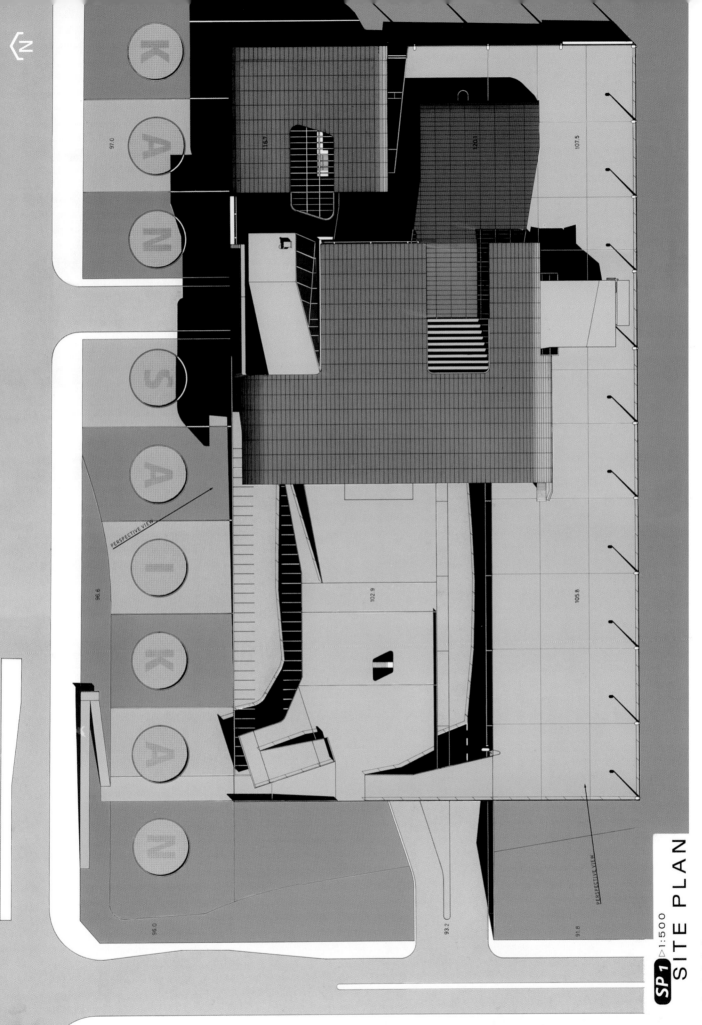

PERSPECTIVE VIEW

PERSPECTIVE VIEW

97.0

96.6

116.7

102.9

120.1

107.5

105.8

96.0

93.2

91.8

K A N S A I K A N

E03 ▷1:300
EAST ELEVATION

関西館

E02 ▷1:300
NORTH ELEVATION

E 04 ▷1:300
WEST ELEVATION

E 01 1:300
SOUTH ELEVATION

View of reading room

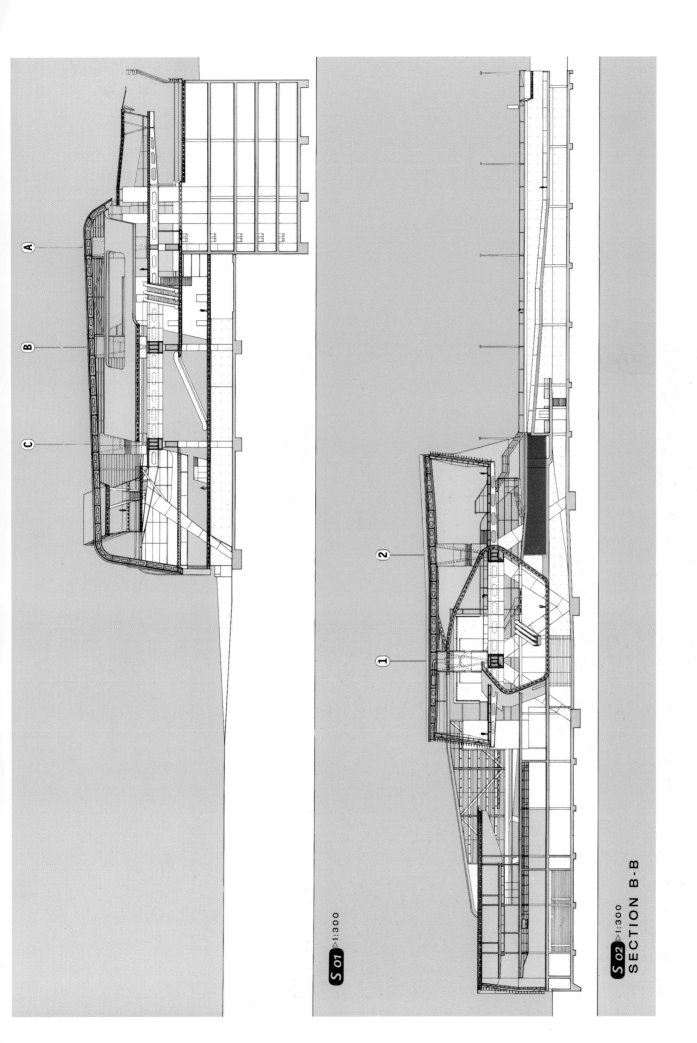

S 01 ▷1:300

S 02 ▷1:300
SECTION B-B

View of entrances

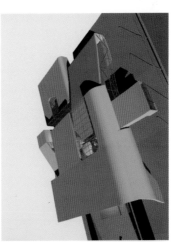

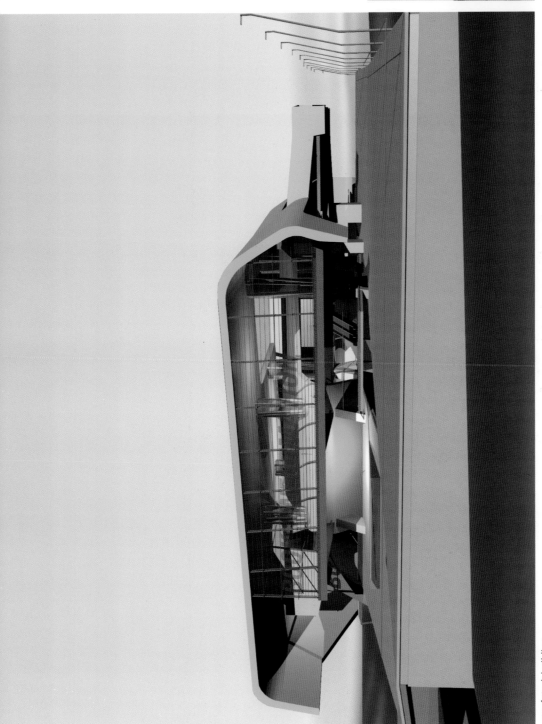

Views of stack building

Koizumi Birdhouse

Project No. 9305
Anywhere
1993

This project was commissioned by the Koizumi Sangyo Company of Osaka, Japan, in 1993. The company asked four architects—Tadao Ando, Neil Denari, Peter Eisenman, and Daniel Libeskind—to make a conceptual project that might confront the continuing ecological crisis by exploring the human/nature problem or presumed dialectic.

The birdhouse is a collision of the poetic fragility of the bird in its line of flight and the degraded consciousness of society in the pleasurized landscape. In a post-Darwinian world of distorted laws of natural selection, we know that the animal world, through survival techniques, has redescribed to us a new concept of limits. Where technology is often derided as the culprit in the ecological crisis we now endure, the misunderstanding of such a critique, by those who create it and those who argue against it, is really the problematic condition.

Through direct means, the concept (myth) of nature as an unlimited landscape is identified by green foam, which is bounded and held up by a mobilized, aluminum arm. This floating patch of the "green" artificial plasmic (molded) landscape forms the floor or ground to the space of the birdhouse, itself suspended in air. The supplemental condition of technology, in the reproduction of the soft ground, argues for a complicit and efficacious way of engaging with what we otherwise recognize as first-degree nature. Inside the birdhouse, bright blue foam, a material made to last five hundred years, covers the declinated vertical surfaces. This repetitively undulating soft surface refers to the space of water and sky , the moment where the Cartesian reference system gives way to the play between the smooth and the striated.

Project No. 9105
Anywhere
1991

Dematerialization

The centuries-old yet still unbelievable production of a transparent material from opaque origins has given the material world an invisible but solid substance: glass. It is curious how this phrase might easily describe the electronic landscape, which, too, is fabricated from the disappearances of certain realities. With the advent of fiber-optic technology, sound and images are able to flow through glass wire with little or no resistance, literally at the speed of light. The house proposed here is concerned less with the vision of glass and more with the speed of the "material" it transmits: light.

Like the surface of the window itself, the sonic/optical resonation of the television monitor (or other projecting system) gives substance a form we call the view. Thus, we are now witness to the changes in our perception of the world around us—a denatured reality within a continuously changing morphological boundary.

Fiber Blobs

Irregular form-vessels skinned in translucent fiberglass cloth are inflated and sustained by the impulses of electronic communication flowing through the house's fiber-optic neural network, which runs between the elements of the structural frame. These envelopes are sensitized and therefore respond to another form of technology.

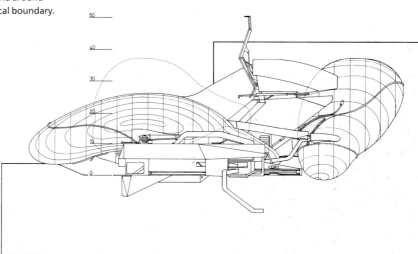

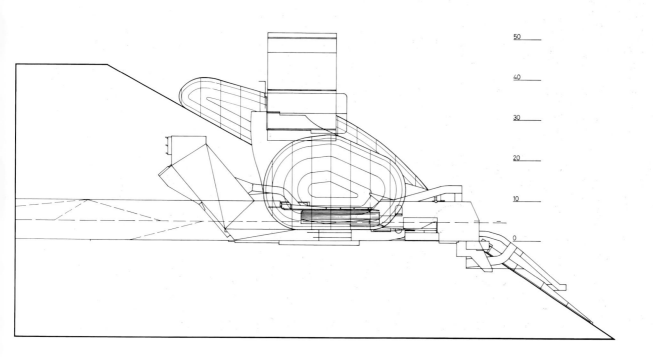

Floating Illuminator

Project No. 9201
Anywhere
1992

Light Geometry
Suspended from above, this object contains five light sources of varying degrees of intensity and quality. They are controlled by a hand-held remote unit that also operates as a rheostat and signaling device. A heat sensor activates the object within an 8-foot range. It is considered to be a floating fragment of a building.

The Illuminator is constructed from break-formed 1-millimeter steel sheet and 8-millimeter aluminum rod with injection-molded plastic reflector.

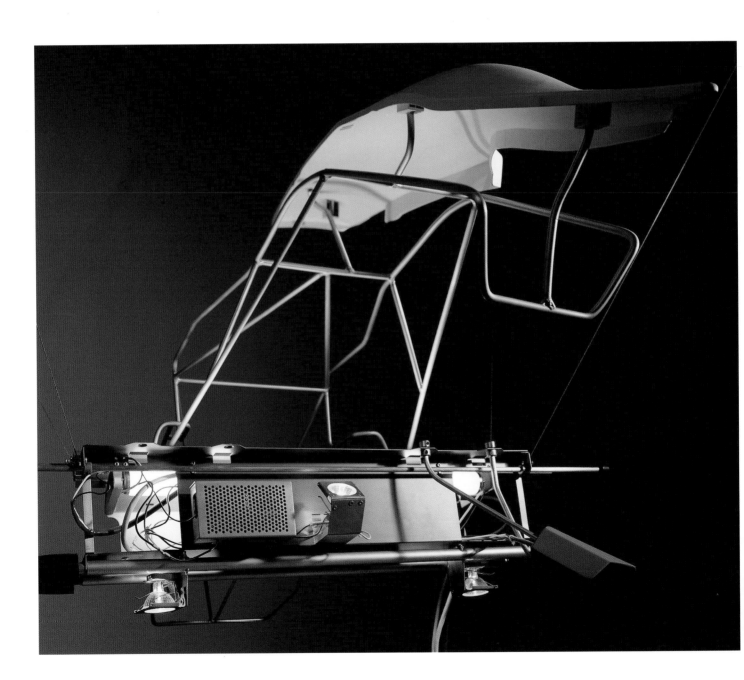

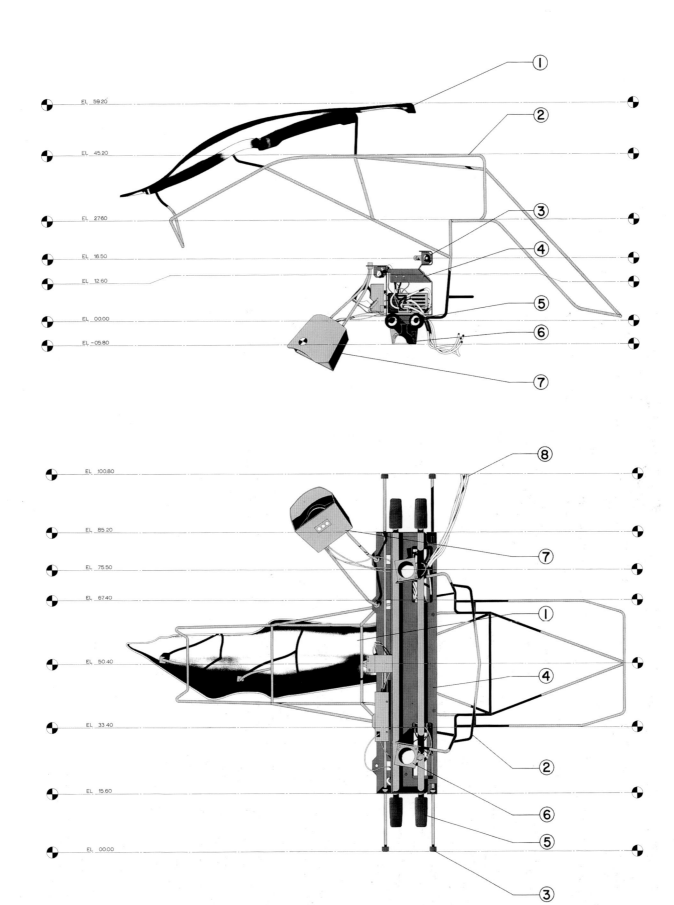

EL 59.20

EL 45.20

EL 27.60

EL 16.50

EL 12.60

EL 00.00

EL −05.80

①
②
③
④
⑤
⑥
⑦

⑧

EL 100.80

EL 85.20

EL 75.50

EL 67.40

EL 50.40

EL 33.40

EL 15.60

EL 00.00

⑦
①
④
②
⑥
⑤
③

Chronology of Projects

Project No. 8201 Conversations with the Sun
Location: Anywhere
Program: A meditation on light
Client: Research project

Project No. 8304 HI-WA House
Location: On the median strip of any freeway in the Southwestern section of the United States (as depicted, I-10 near Los Angeles)
Program: Single-family house vertically deployed, including swimming pool, gym, and chapel. A speculation on upward mobility.
Client: Shinkenchiku Residential Competition

Project No. 8303-4 Monastery NYC
Location: Eighth Avenue at 20th Street, Chelsea, New York, New York
Program: Urban monastery, refuge, and asylum for city dwellers
Client: Research project

Project No. 8407 Adam's House in Paradise
Location: Eldridge Street, Lower East Side, New York, New York
Program: Low-cost housing inspired by the work of Adam Purple, a local squatters' rights and nature activist
Client: Sponsored by the StoreFront for Art and Architecture, New York, New York

Project No. 8501 Heuristic Structures
Location: Anywhere
Program: Spatial studies following the precepts suggested in the book *The Laws of Form* by G. Spencer Brown
Client: Research project

Project No. 8602 Solar Clock
Location: On top of the perimeter wall at the Tower of London, adjacent to the Tower Bridge and the Thames River
Program: A large solar-powered events machine and analog clock vehicle
Client: Project created for an exhibition entitled "The London Project," a group show by ten young architects, held at Artists' Space in New York City in 1988

Project No. 8606 Public School Prototype
Location: Bronx, New York
Program: K–6 public school
Client: Research project

Project No. 8708 Leesburg City Hall Competition
Location: Leesburg, Virginia
Program: City Hall facilities and town square for a town of 60,000 located 30 miles east of Washington, D.C.
Client: Competition

Project No. CP-8706 Exploding Sonic Test Audio Visual Big Guitar
Location: Anywhere
Program: The Big Guitar is a spatial-interactive piece that explores the roots of the guitar culturally as well as physically. It is a large aluminum resonator box, which the player occupies. It is the scale of the body, between the size of the guitar and a room. Upon entering, the viewer faces the neck, six 10-foot-long strings supported by a fret board, and an oscilloscope at an elevation of 5 feet, 2 inches. Any space is automatically an acoustical container of sounds, the theater or symphony hall being the most specialized in shape. Any change of that space's size and shape affects what we hear. The Big Guitar uses an interactive rotating roof flap that alters the small space in which the player is enclosed. The fixed edges of the

space are designed to reflect sound down to the player, generating unpredictable geometrical reverberation patterns. Volume, tone, and roof controls may be operated while viewing the sine curve display of the oscilloscope — the visual representation of the frequencies generated by setting the strings into a vibratory motion.
Client: Sponsored by Columbia University, the Big Guitar was a project included in an exhibition entitled "Installed Mechanisms."
Project Team: Neil Denari, Mark Brearley, Peter Cook, Larry Davis, Diana Thater, Hisham Youseff

Project No. 8712 Astronauts' Memorial Competition
Location: Kennedy Space Center, Florida
Program: Memorial for all astronauts who lost their lives in the NASA Space Program
Client: Competition sponsored by NASA
Project Team: Neil Denari, Masaaki Oka

Project No. 8805 West Coast Gateway Competition: Phases 1 (Finalist) and 2
Location: Spanning the 101 Freeway in downtown Los Angeles, California
Program: A 36-million-dollar project for the celebration of the multicultural foundation of Los Angeles as represented by the accomplishments and positive actions of the millions of immigrants to the city in the twentieth century. This "global village" was captured in a program consisting of cinemas, galleries, international restaurants, libraries, and cultural offices.
Client: Competition sponsored by the West Coast Gateway Commission
Project Team: Neil Denari, Alec Kobayashi, Mathias Tinner, Steve Lacap, Scott Romses, Kazem Naderi
Associate Architect: Dworsky Associates, Los Angeles

Project No. 8803–4 Minimum House Prototype No. 1
Location: Prototypical rear yard site, intended to replace existing detached garages
Program: Small multi-use dwelling with two-car parking. Only 20 feet square in the groundplan (the size of a typical two-car garage), this three-level house is designed as a totally prefabricated unit that accommodates by being more vertical than horizontal. The minimum footprint responds to the conservation of land (the ground of the city) while remaining autonomous. The interior spaces are unnamed in terms of use. It is projected as both a starter house and as a backyard extension deployed within a conventional housing situation.
Client: Research project

Project No. 8902 Pool Regenerator
Location: Empty public swimming pool in Hollywood, California
Program: Public events space as a reprogramming of the existing void-space of the pool
Client: Research project

Project No. 8906 FIELD—Feynman Institute for Experimental Laboratory Developments
Location: California Institute of Technology, Pasadena, California
Program: Research facility for Cal Tech's theoretical physics department
Client: Research project
Project Team: Neil Denari, Pornchai Boonsom

Project No. 8910 Tokyo International Forum Competition (Third Prize)
Location: On a site in the Marunouchi district, Tokyo, Japan, formerly the site of Kenzo Tange's Tokyo City Hall building from the 1950s
Program: 100,000 square meters of mixed-use public facilities, including three large auditoriums, information salons, exhibition halls, and meeting rooms. The program as given is essentially void of any significant meaning in cultural

terms. To build a project of such a size in a city where there is no more (free) space is the spatial paradox that drives the scheme. Volumetric expression is generated from the phenomenal aspects of acoustics, light, movement, and the complete dissipation of straightforward structuring systems such as circulation or vertical support. Given the suspension of these regularized datums, the course taken sought out inefficiencies and discrepancies of use as a zone of formal experimentation.
Client: Competition sponsored by the city of Tokyo.
Project Team: Neil Denari, Yasuyuki Okazaki, Masaaki Oka, Alec Kobayashi, Steve Lacap, Eric Altizer

Project No. 9003 Details Design Studio (Schemes 1–4)
Location: A 2,000-square-foot loft space in SoHo, New York
Program: A "wall" to divide a single space into two distinct functions for a small industrial design company, including book and model storage and a foldout work space.
Client: Details, a division of Steelcase, Incorporated
Project Team: Neil Denari, Pornchai Boonsom

Project No. 9004 Entropy Machine
Location: The densified air above the city
Program: Aluminum structure with rotating monokote-blue flaps that conceptually describe the continuous motion of communications entropy
Client: Sponsored by the Japan Association for the Promotion of Events; exhibited at the Tepia Building, Tokyo
Project Team: Neil Denari, Alec Kobayashi

Project No. 9005 Six Los Angeles Protosites
Location: Los Angeles, California
Program: Sloping hillsides, flat grids, valley edges, boulevard spans, and high-rise penthouses are explored as prototypical and repeating site conditions.
Client: Research project
Project Team: Neil Denari, Alec Kobayashi

Project No. 9007 World Library Prototype
Location: Anywhere
Program: A schematic design based on the production, sales, distribution, and storage of the book. Two linear factory wings, one fiction and one nonfiction, automatically design, print, and bind any given number of books when ordered through drive-up service. The manuscripts are sent directly to the library through a computer network that bypasses the usual editorial and publication processes. All books are stored on CD-ROM disks and can be accessed and printed at any moment for sales to the general public, essentially turning the library into a collision of the specific programs of a bookstore and the Library of Congress. Because the project is a prototype, and meant to be repeated, the collection in Alkmaar, Holland, for instance, could be similar to the ones in Osaka or St. Louis. Translation of material denies a strictly regional collection.
Client: Research project
Project Team: Neil Denari, Pornchai Boonsom

Project No. 9009 Prototype Landscape
Location: Los Angeles periphery, Southern California
Program: Made up of circulation corridors, restricted zones of power supply (and military research), accessible zones of natural and unnatural landscapes, and gridded textures of housing set against the mirage of the nascent desertscape, the Southern California landscape is a distortion (louder and fuzzier) of American expansionism. With a degree of planning that is essentially spatially dystopic at all speeds, roads may go through buildings, artificial ground planes may connect and disconnect, geometries may act like the camouflage painted on the airplanes con-

structed nearby, and nature may be bounded by architecture so it can be used as a photosynthetic device, a kind of soft machinery intended not to visually humanize the place but rather to compensate for the stale biomechanics of building.
Client: Research project
Project Team: Neil Denari, Pornchai Boonsom

Project No. 9011 Tokyo JR Subway Competition
Location: Tokyo subway system, Japan
Program: Design of three separate stations for the JR system. Length, platform dimensions, and structural conditions are given.
Client: Japan Railroad
Project Team: Neil Denari, Ken Yamaguchi, Yasuyuki Okazaki, Masaaki Oka, Shin Ozawa

Project No. 9015 The Computer: Architecture of the Nonrigid Body
Location: Anywhere
Program: A graphic meditation on the symbolic formal logic of the computer
Client: Research project

Project No. 9101 Exhibition Design/Tokyo Cipher
Location: Axis Building, Tokyo, Japan
Program: Installation design for the student work completed in a SCI-Arc and Shibaura Institute of Technology joint design studio held in Tokyo. Within this exhibition, entitled "Metropolis in Transition," the Tokyo Cipher was suspended in air and operated as an architectural character whose meaning is "pacific space."
Client: Inspiration Gallery, Tokyo
Contractor: Yamagiwa Lighting Company

Project No. 9102 Intransigencies and Paralogics
Location: On video
Program: A collaboration with James Ludwig, industrial designer and architect; a thirty-minute video in five parts exploring beauty, function, meaning, language, and form in contemporary technology
Client: New York City chapter of the American Institute of Architects
Project Team: Neil Denari, James Ludwig, Pornchai Boonsom

Project No. 9103 Caravan Prototype
Location: Anywhere
Program: Within a standard 5.3-meter-long caravan size, develop a concept prototype that would advance the technology and functions of the mass-produced caravan and challenge the relationship between design and industry. From the original length, the exterior lightweight fiberglass skin splits apart to extend to 8.5 meters. Additionally, the front nosecone folds out with an extended lounge chair inside this space. Two bays, framed by aluminum structure, are revealed. One section is the service core, which is skinned with a black-and-white pattern, a geometrical distortion of the frame itself. The other bay is all glass and unfolds toward the landscape beyond.
Client: Museum of Contemporary Art, Sydney; Craig Bremner, curator
Contractor: Jayco Manufacturing, Melbourne
Project Team: Neil Denari, Wyndham Chow, with Masaaki Oka, Benny Chan, Laurence Turner

→

Project No. 9105 Fiber-glasfibre House
Location: Anywhere
Program: Explore a technologically advanced house utilizing fiber optics, super-HVAC, and supple envelopes of fiberglass.
Client: Unsubmitted entry for the Shinkenchiku "Another Glass House" Competition
Project Team: Neil Denari, Kaspar Baumeister

Project No. 9201 Floating Illuminator
Location: Anywhere
Program: Suspended lighting structure
Client: Gallery of Functional Art, Santa Monica, California
Project Team: Neil Denari, Laurence Turner, Kostas Manolides

Project No. 9203 Kawasaki Void Competition
Location: The 32nd floor of the Kawasaki Heavy Industry Headquarters in Kobe, Japan
Program: The building itself is a 33-level reflective glass object without strong characteristics. This kind of building is a typical design by Nikken Sekkei, commonly referred to as the Japanese SOM. At the 31st floor, the building has a void space, the only strong identity of the building, but neither the architects nor the clients have any ideas about how to use or develop it. Therefore, no specific program was given.

The subtext of the competition, Kawasaki's difficulty with being a high-tech company riddled with environmental concerns, makes the problem of corporate identity an ambiguous one. At what expense to the idea of nature is technological progress being carried out? How is the civilized domain of the city an inevitable restructuring of nature? In using the constant 30 kilometers/hour wind velocity, two information projectiles operate on wind-generated power, each installed with a cylindrical turbine system. The nosecones move horizontally on tracks hanging from the structure above, violating the vertical plane of the building. Once beyond the plane of the glass curtain wall, an information fin unfolds to project and receive images, color, light, text, and so on to and from the city of Kobe. The movement of the pieces is connected to a computer system that controls the information systems within the building. Given that these systems are in use twenty-four hours a day, monitored both by people and by the internal memories of the system program, the information projectiles move sporadically and at varying speeds. Between the animated elements is a glass space set up as a small bar, allowing the visitor to experience the disorienting effects of alcohol and technology.
Client: Invited competition sponsored by Kawasaki Heavy Industries
Project Team: Neil Denari, Laurence Turner, Kostas Manolides, Kevin Southerland, Juan Garcia

Project No. 9204 Prototype Schools (Schemes 1–5)
Location: Southern California
Program: High school featuring computer-based learning
Client: Research project

Project No. 9205 Desert Center
Location: Lancaster, California
Program: Community center
Client: Research project
Project Team: Neil Denari, Tomoharu Ono, Benny Chan, Eric Chen

Project No. 9303 Prototype House
Location: Setagaya-ku, Tokyo, Japan
Program: Three-level single-family house
Client: Research project
Project Team: Neil Denari, Benny Chan, Tomoharu Ono, Hiroki Aso

Project No. 9304 Details Design Studio
final scheme; see Project No. 9003 for description
Project Team: Neil Denari, Benny Chan, David Hsu

Project No. 9305 Koizumi Birdhouse
Location: Anywhere
Program: Conceptual birdhouse
Client: Koizumi Sangyo Co.
Project Team: Neil Denari, Tomoharu Ono, Benny Chan

Project No. 9307 Museum of the Twentieth Century (Third Prize)
Location: Los Angeles International Airport
Program: Ten exhibition halls for the display of the century's artifacts and images
Client: Central Glass Ideas Competition, Tokyo, Japan

Project No. 9309 Morsiglia Housing and Study Center
Location: Village of Morsiglia, Cap Corse, Corsica
Program: Twenty units of student and visitor apartments, a nature study center, a soccer field
Client: Eco-Tec, New York City and Morsiglia

Project No. 9405 Massey Residence (Schnitt-Haus)
Location: West side of Los Angeles, California
Program: 2,700-square-foot single-family house with swimming pool
Client: Richard Massey
Project Team: Neil Denari and Andrew Waisler with Yutaka Matsumoto, Masao Yahagi

Project No. 9406 Yokohama Port Terminal Competition
Location: 483-meter-long pier in Yokohama/Tokyo Bay, Japan
Program: 48,000-square-meter cruise ship terminal for up to four liners with departure and arrival halls, information center, customs and immigration, and cruise deck
Client: Competition sponsored by the Yokohama Port Authority
Project Team: Neil Denari, Yutaka Matsumoto, Tomoharu Ono, Benny Chan, Kaspar Baumeister, Richard Massey (graphic design)

Project No. 9501 Tokyo Minimum High-Rise Housing
Location: Tokyo, Japan
Program: Seven efficiency apartments and two public bars in an eleven-level tower
Client: Nippon Housing International, Ltd.
Project Team: Neil Denari, Irene Lai, Gunther Schatz, John Hartmann, Angus Schoenberger

Project No. 9503 Sprawl Connectors
Location: Los Angeles, California
Program: Large-scale drive-through complexes. In any city, circulation is perhaps the most important aspect of infrastructural systems. Money, water, electricity, automobiles, media images, information, and so on are all circulating phenomena. Concurrent to the concept of movement are speed, time, and distance. These aerial view drawings are speculations about the concept of connecting the city grid to the systems of circulation that cut through the city in the high-speed corridors. Like the freeway on-off ramp, a space of deceleration and acceleration, the large buildings are designed to incorporate many rates of movement and circulation into a single but multispatial volume.
Client: Research project

Project No. 9504 OC-EX-CEN
Location: Irvine, California
Program: Orange County Exhibition Center
Client: Research project

Project No. 9601 Interrupted Projections
Location: Gallery MA, Nogizaka, Tokyo, Japan
Program: A 75-square-meter temporary experimental space
Client: Gallery MA/Toto Co., Ltd.
Project Team: Neil Denari, Raita Nakajima, Georg Kolmayr, Duks Koschitz,
Jimmy Miyoshi
Producers: Masaaki Oka, Sei'ichi Kozu (associated architect)
Contractor: Iriki

Project No. 9605 Arlington Museum of Art
Location: Arlington, Texas, which is on the center line between Dallas and
Fort Worth in the Dallas–Fort Worth Metroplex
Program: Renovation of an existing 20,000-square-foot contemporary art center,
development of an adjacent park space, and the design of a new 3,200-square-foot
addition for exhibition
Client: Joan Davidow, director, Arlington Museum of Art
Project Team: Neil Denari, Thad Reeves, Angus Schoenberger, Jeremy Limsenben,
with Gunther Schatz, John Hartmann, Fred Meyer, Masako Fujinami

Project No. 9602 Kansai-kan Library Competition
Location: In the Keihanna Hills between Kyoto and Osaka, Japan
Program: A 60,000-square-meter nonlending research repository. Half of the
program accommodates stacks while the other consists of large reading rooms,
administration, and exhibition halls. Some 200 meters long, the site is also to
be developed as an open public plaza space.
Client: Competition sponsored by the National Diet Library, Japan
Project Team: Neil Denari, Masao Yahagi, Tomoharu Ono, Tomohiro Miyashita,
Tsuyoshi Horie, Georg Kolmayr

Project No. 9704 Vertical Smoothouse
Location: Los Angeles, California
Program: Proposal for a three-level, two-bedroom efficiency dwelling with
parking and exterior deck
Client: [withheld]
Project Team: Neil Denari, Carsten Primdahl, John Hartmann, Andrew Waisler,
Rebecca Rudolph

Project No. 9705 NMDA Offices
Location: Los Angeles, California
Program: 600-square-foot office for Neil M. Denari Architects
Project Team: Neil Denari, Rebecca Rudolph, John Hartmann, Troy Ostrander,
Chris Pfiffner
Builder: Robert Brock

Project No. 9706 Microsoft.SF
Location: San Francisco, California
Program: Conceptual design for a 1,000-square-meter interior retail store for
Microsoft, the first of its kind
Client: A joint venture of Microsoft, Inc., and Sony Development, Burbank

Project Team: Neil Denari, Andrew Waisler with Rob Letterman, Anders Beer,
Angus Schoenberger
Associate Architect: Richard Altuna (retail strategist)
Graphics: Weiden + Kennedy, Portland, Oregon (Whitney Lowe, project designer)

Project No. 9802 Technology Research Park
Location: Agoura Hills, California
Program: 10,000-square-meter office and laboratory building for high-technology
companies
Client: Research project
Project Team: Neil Denari, Andrew Waisler, Troy Ostrander

Project No. 9803 Multisection Office Block
Location: Los Angeles, California
Program: 350,000 square feet of office space and related commercial lease space
Client: Research project
Project Team: Neil Denari, Friedrich Tuzcek, Jae Shin

Project No. 9804 Corrugated Duct House
Location: Palm Springs, California
Program: 2,700-square-foot house with swimming pool
Client: [withheld]
Project Team: Neil Denari, Jae Shin

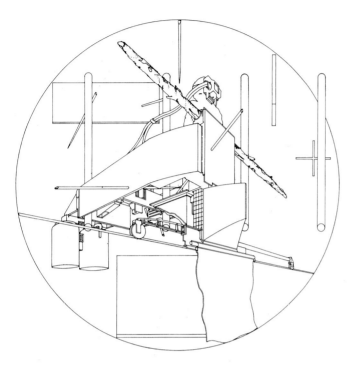

CONVERSATIONS W/ THE SUN

PARIS 1982

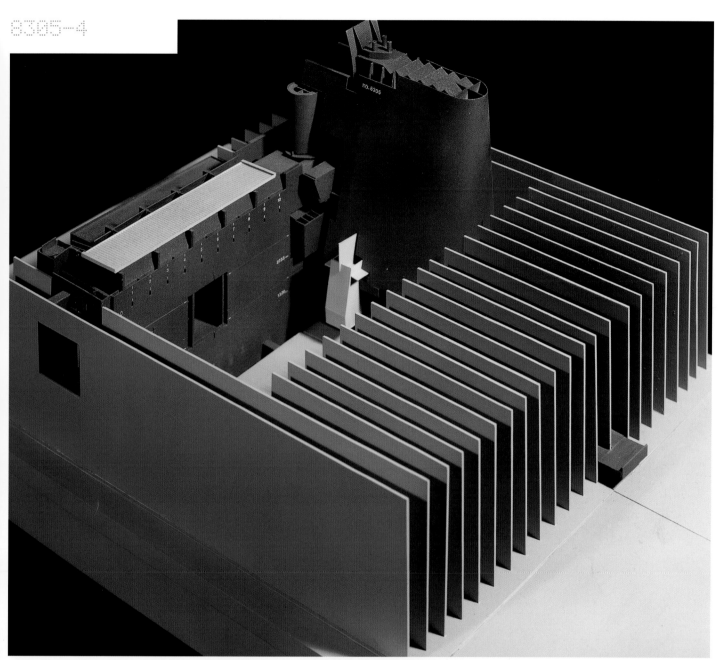

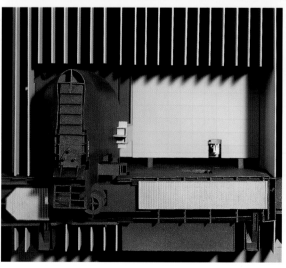

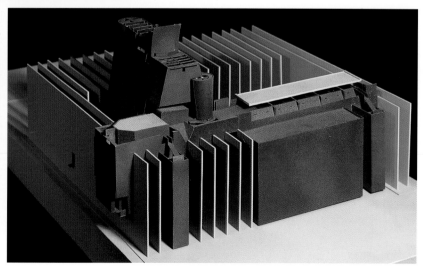

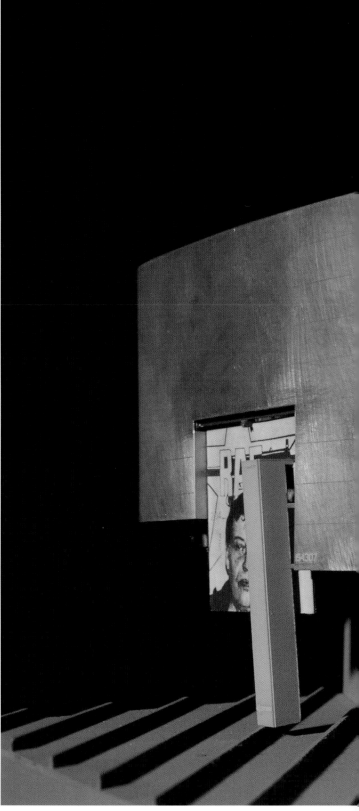

EXPLODING SONIC TEST AUDIO VISUAL BIG GUITAR   CP-8706

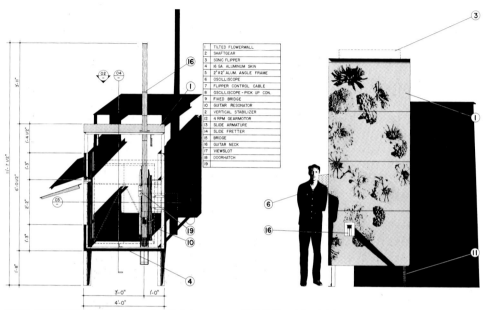

1	TILTED FLOWERWALL
2	SHAFTGEAR
3	SONIC FLIPPER
4	16 GA. ALUMINUM SKIN
5	2"X2" ALUM. ANGLE FRAME
6	OSCILLISCOPE
7	FLIPPER CONTROL CABLE
8	OSCILLOSCOPE - PICK UP CON.
9	FIXED BRIDGE
10	GUITAR RESONATOR
11	VERTICAL STABILIZER
12	4 RPM GEARMOTOR
13	SLIDE ARMATURE
14	SLIDE FRETTER
15	BRIDGE
16	GUITAR NECK
17	VIEWSLOT
18	DOORHATCH
19	

Fig. CP-01—Horizontal Section (Top View). The amplified frequency of the vibrating strings resonates within the aluminum sounding box. The instruments length is intended to produce the largest possible harmonic cycle of the fundamental.

Fig. CP-02—Flowerwall (Front view). The projected wall deflects the sound energy down toward the player. Harmonious or discordant tones may be produced by unison or random tunings of the six six strings. The vibration of the aluminum skin deepens the bass range harmonics.

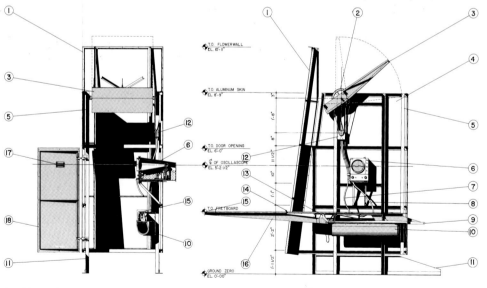

Fig. CP-03—Vertical Section. The energy withheld in a musical instrument is usually expended in setting the air around it into vibration. it is only through its steady discharge of energy into the surrounding air that we hear the instrument at all : The electric pick-up recieves this disturbance of air over a magnetic pole which then generates the electronic signal.

Fig. CP-04—Vertical Section. The signal is then heard through amplification and seen as the oscilliscope produces the sine curve in response to the frequency of the signal. The sound curve of a musical sound is periodic, it recurs at perfectly regular intervals. It is essentially a graphic display of the actual vibrating string with the waves traveling along its length.

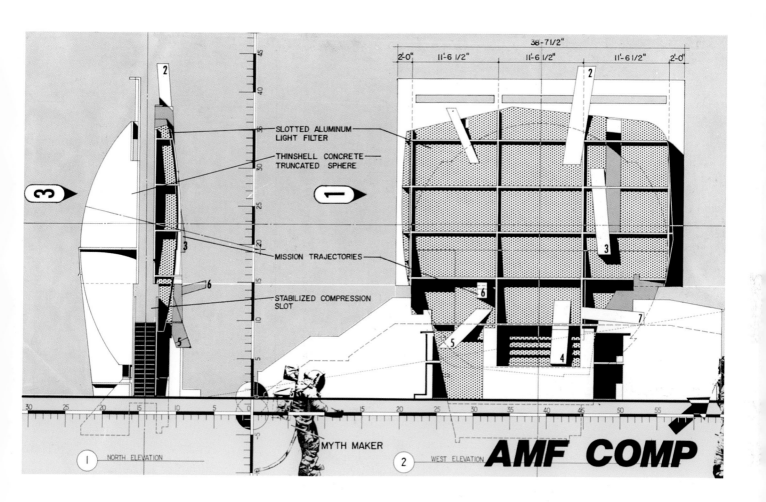

SLOTTED ALUMINUM
LIGHT FILTER

THINSHELL CONCRETE
TRUNCATED SPHERE

MISSION TRAJECTORIES

STABILIZED COMPRESSION
SLOT

38-71/2"

2'-0"   11'-6 1/2"   11'-6 1/2"   11'-6 1/2"   2'-0"

MYTH MAKER

① NORTH ELEVATION

② WEST ELEVATION   **AMF COMP**

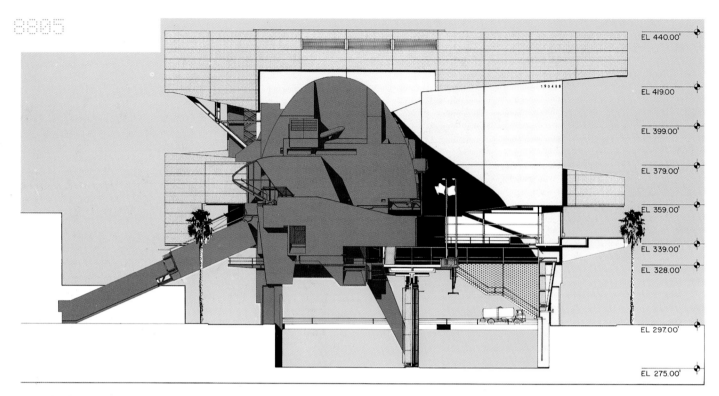

no. WG08 SOUTHEAST ELEVATION (BI) | | | | | IOI NORTH

EL 440.00'
EL 419.00
EL 399.00'
EL 379.00'
EL 359.00'
EL 339.00'
EL 328.00'
EL 297.00'
EL 275.00'

LOS ANGELES 1988

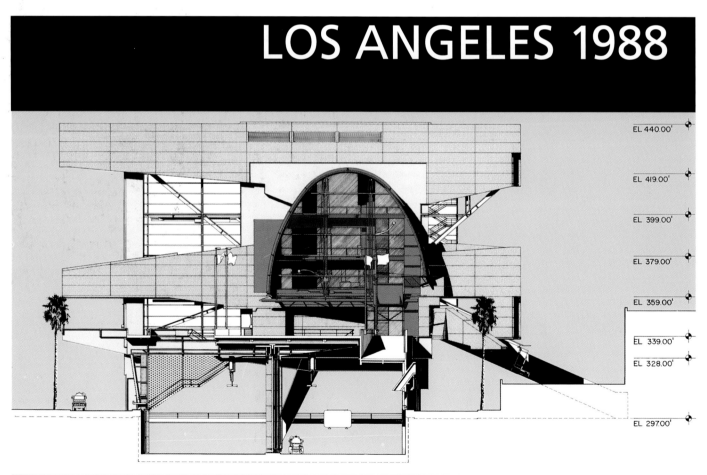

EL 440.00'
EL 419.00'
EL 399.00'
EL 379.00'
EL 359.00'
EL 339.00'
EL 328.00'
EL 297.00'

no. WG09 NORTHWEST ELEVATION (BI) | | | | IOI SOUTH

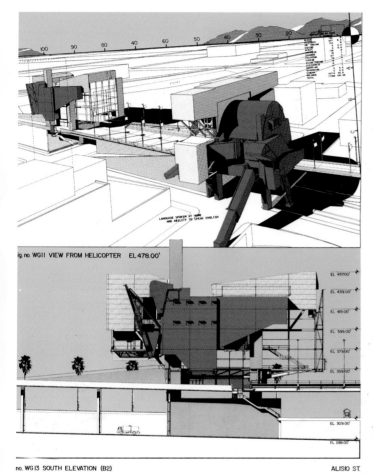

fig. no. WG11 VIEW FROM HELICOPTER EL 478.00'

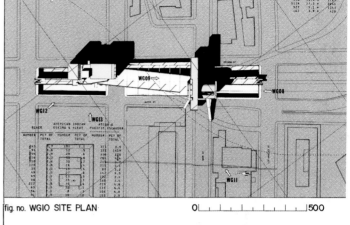

fig. no. WG10 SITE PLAN

0 |_|_|_|_|_| 500

no. WG13 SOUTH ELEVATION (B2)   ALISIO ST.

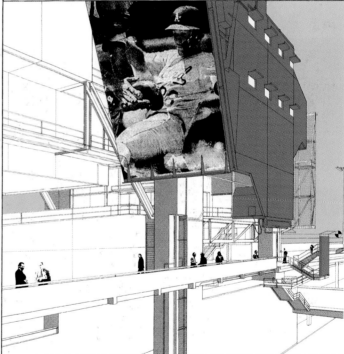

fig. no. WG12 ENTRANCE (B2)

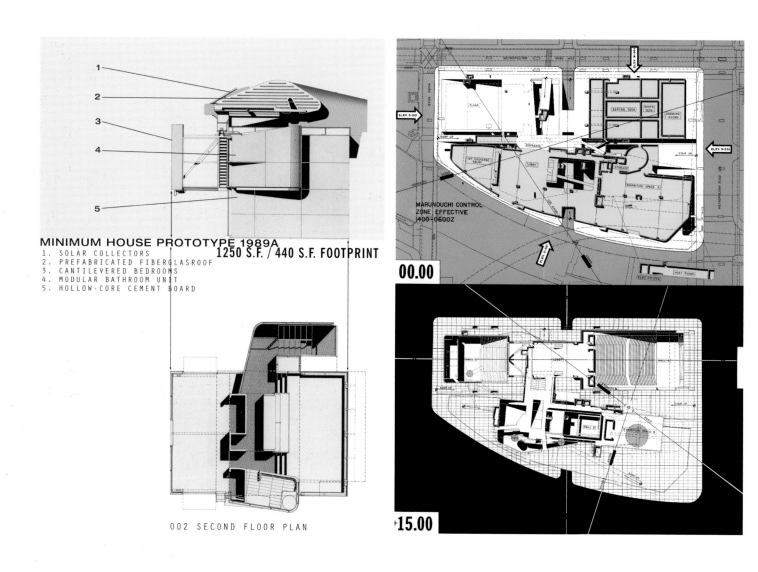

MINIMUM HOUSE PROTOTYPE 1989A
1250 S.F. / 440 S.F. FOOTPRINT
1. SOLAR COLLECTORS
2. PREFABRICATED FIBERGLASROOF
3. CANTILEVERED BEDROOMS
4. MODULAR BATHROOM UNIT
5. HOLLOW-CORE CEMENT BOARD

002 SECOND FLOOR PLAN

MARUNOUCHI CONTROL
ZONE EFFECTIVE
1400-0600Z

00.00

+15.00

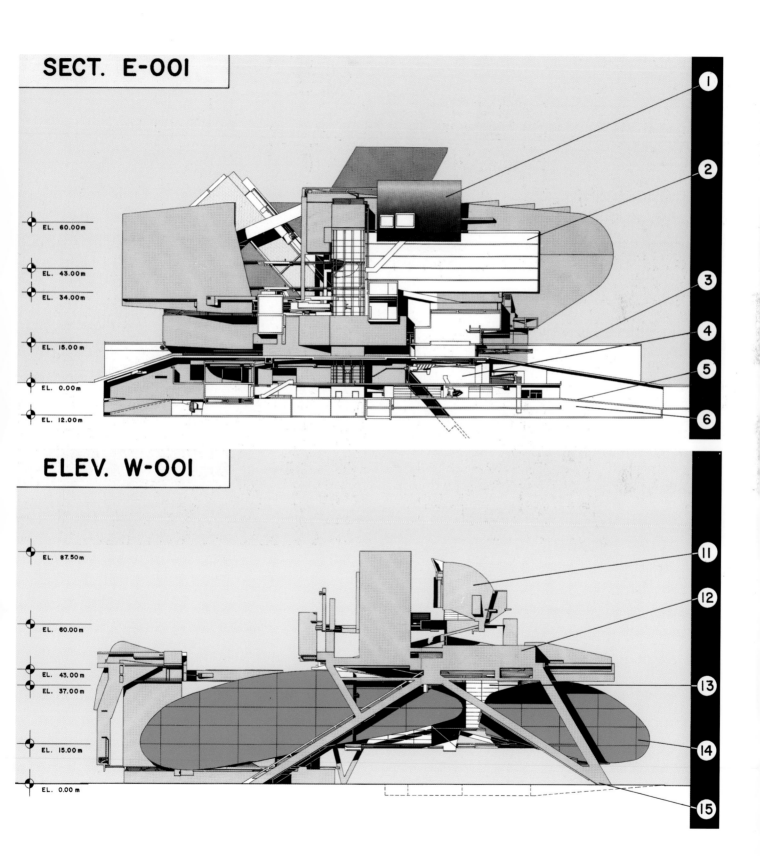

SECT. E-001

EL. 60.00 m
EL. 43.00 m
EL. 34.00 m
EL. 15.00 m
EL. 0.00 m
EL. 12.00 m

1
2
3
4
5
6

ELEV. W-001

EL. 87.50 m
EL. 60.00 m
EL. 43.00 m
EL. 37.00 m
EL. 15.00 m
EL. 0.00 m

11
12
13
14
15

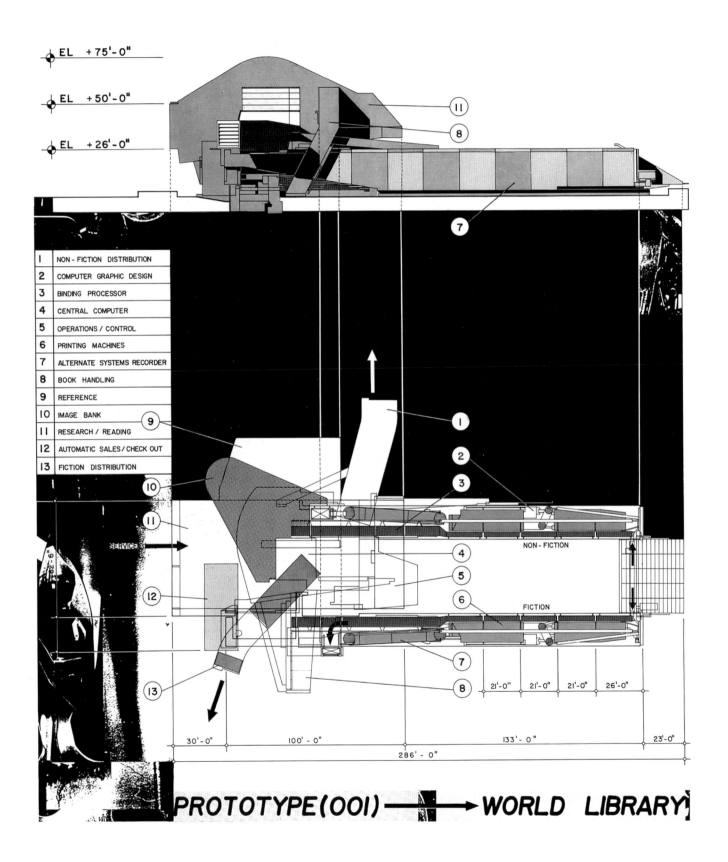

1	NON - FICTION DISTRIBUTION
2	COMPUTER GRAPHIC DESIGN
3	BINDING PROCESSOR
4	CENTRAL COMPUTER
5	OPERATIONS / CONTROL
6	PRINTING MACHINES
7	ALTERNATE SYSTEMS RECORDER
8	BOOK HANDLING
9	REFERENCE
10	IMAGE BANK
11	RESEARCH / READING
12	AUTOMATIC SALES / CHECK OUT
13	FICTION DISTRIBUTION

EL +75'-0"
EL +50'-0"
EL +26'-0"

NON - FICTION

FICTION

SERVICE

21'-0" 21'-0" 21'-0" 26'-0"

30'-0"   100'-0"   133'-0"   23'-0"

286'-0"

PROTOTYPE (001) ⟶ WORLD LIBRARY

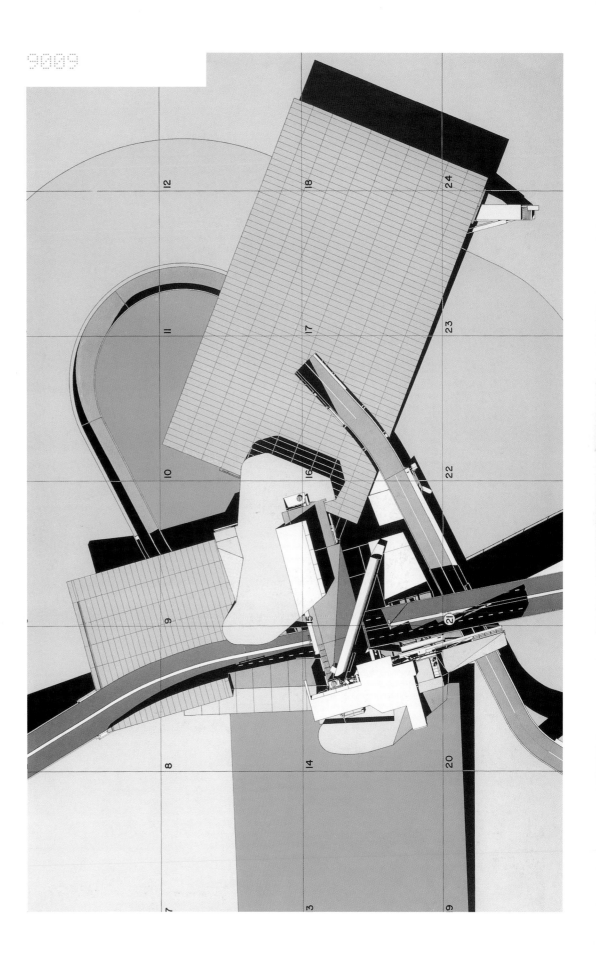

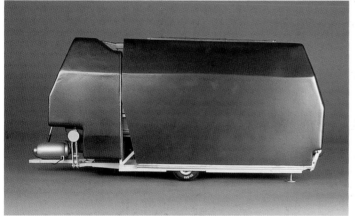

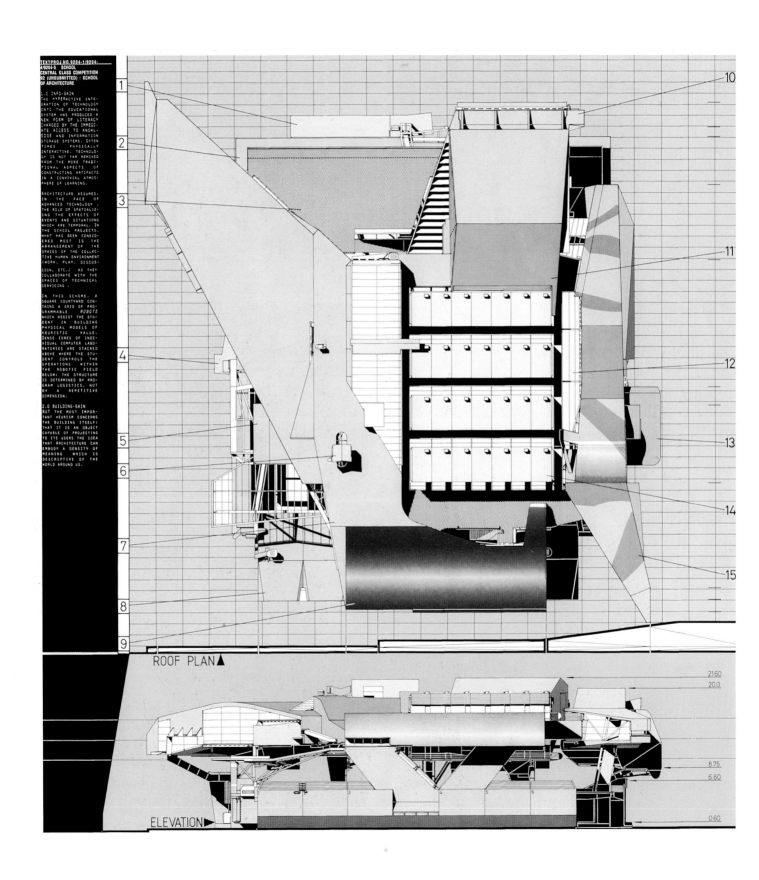

TEXTPROJ.NO.9204-1/9204-4/9204-5 SCHOOL
CENTRAL GLASS COMPETITION
92 (UNSUBMITTED) : SCHOOL
OF ARCHITECTURE

1.0 INFO-GAIN
THE HYPERACTIVE INTE-
GRATION OF TECHNOLOGY
INTO THE EDUCATIONAL
SYSTEM HAS PRODUCED A
NEW FORM OF LITERACY
CHARGED BY THE IMMEDI-
ATE ACCESS TO KNOWL-
EDGE AND INFORMATION
STORAGE SYSTEMS. OFTEN
TIMES PHYSICALLY
INTERACTIVE, TECHNOLO-
GY IS NOT FAR REMOVED
FROM THE MORE TRADI-
TIONAL ASPECTS OF
CONSTRUCTING ARTIFACTS
IN A CONVIVIAL ATMOS-
PHERE OF LEARNING.

ARCHITECTURE ASSUMES,
IN THE FACE OF
ADVANCED TECHNOLOGY ,
THE ROLE OF SPATIALIZ-
ING THE EFFECTS OF
EVENTS AND SITUATIONS
WHICH ARE TEMPORAL. IN
THE SCHOOL PROJECTS,
WHAT HAS BEEN CONSID-
ERED MOST IS THE
ARRANGEMENT OF THE
SPACES OF THE COLLEC-
TIVE HUMAN ENVIRONMENT
(WORK, PLAY, DISCUS-
SION, ETC.) AS THEY
COLLABORATE WITH THE
SPACES OF TECHNICAL
SERVICING .

IN THIS SCHEME, A
SQUARE COURTYARD CON-
TAINS A GRID OF PRO-
GRAMMABLE *ROBOTS*
WHICH ASSIST THE STU-
DENT IN BUILDING
PHYSICAL MODELS OF
HEURISTIC VALUE.
DENSE CORES OF INDI-
VIDUAL COMPUTER LABO-
RATORIES ARE STACKED
ABOVE WHERE THE STU-
DENT CONTROLS THE
OPERATIONS WITHIN
THE ROBOTIC FIELD
BELOW; THE STRUCTURE
IS DETERMINED BY PRO-
GRAM LOGISTICS, NOT
BY A REPETITIVE
DIMENSION.

2.0 BUILDING-GAIN
BUT THE MOST IMPOR-
TANT HEURISM CONCERNS
THE BUILDING ITSELF:
THAT IT IS AN OBJECT
CAPABLE OF PROJECTING
TO ITS USERS THE IDEA
THAT ARCHITECTURE CAN
EMBODY A DENSITY OF
MEANING WHICH IS
DESCRIPTIVE OF THE
WORLD AROUND US.

ROOF PLAN ▲

ELEVATION ▶

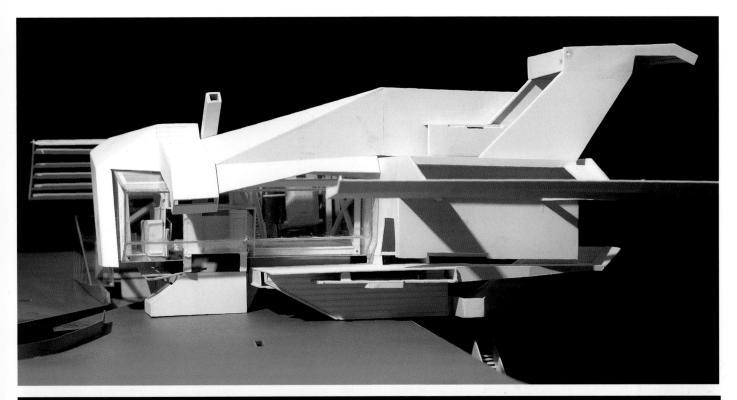

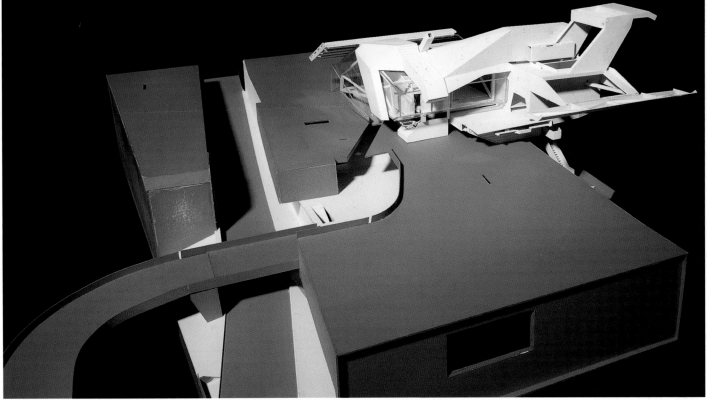

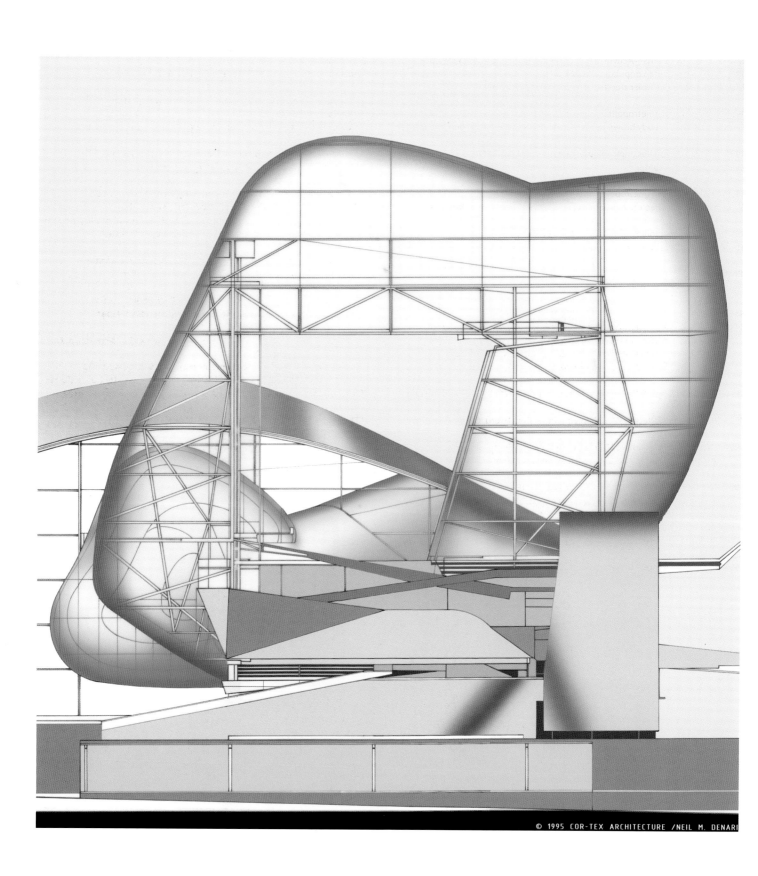

© 1995 COR-TEX ARCHITECTURE /NEIL M. DENARI

Personal Data

NMD Urban Movements—Activities in Cities of More than Ten Million People

1982 Paris (metropolitan population 10,275,000)
Five months of Le Corbusier studies, cuisine, and clay-court tennis

1983–1988 New York (metropolitan population 18,087,251)
Five years of Krylon ruddy brown primer, Glenn Branca, and Sonic Youth

1988–present Los Angeles (metropolitan population 14,531,529)
Eleven years of horizontality

1990–1991, 1992 Tokyo (metropolitan population 30,300,000)
Six months of bubble economy euphoria; two months of post-bubble depression

1994 London (metropolitan population 11,100,000)
Three months of Bartlett conversations

1995 New York
Four months of Avery Library

Solo Exhibitions

1989 "Neil M. Denari: Recent Work," Das Fenster Gallery, Frankfurt, Germany
     "Neil M. Denari: Recent Work," Architecture Gallery, Hamburg, Germany
     "Cor-Tex Projects 1985–1989," 2AES Gallery, San Francisco, California
     "Cor-Tex Projects 1985–1989," StoreFront, New York, New York

1990 "Cor-Tex Projects 1985–1989," University of Houston College of Architecture

1993 "Neil M. Denari: Recent Work," Miami University, Oxford, Ohio

1994 "Osculated Objectiles: Neil Denari, Recent Work," Form Zero
     Architectural Books and Gallery, Los Angeles, California

1995 "Neil Denari," Philippe Uzzon Gallery, Paris, France
     "16hrs: Pacific Deployments—Cor-Tex Projects," Gallery ROM, Oslo, Norway
     "Recent Work," Kansas State University, Manhattan, Kansas

1996 "Interrupted Projections: Cor-Tex Projects," Gallery MA, Tokyo, Japan

1999 "Massey Residence," University of Colorado, Denver, Colorado

Group Exhibitions

1984 "Adam's House in Paradise," StoreFront, New York, New York

1985 "Tradition of Imagination: Neil Denari and Bart Prince," StoreFront,
     New York, New York
     "Independent Visions," StoreFront, New York, New York

1986 "Critical Regionalism: New York," Gallery 400, Chicago, Illinois
     "Building; Machines," P.S. 1, Long Island City, New York

1987 "Installed Mechanisms," Columbia University, New York, New York
1988 "The London Project," Artists Space, New York, New York
     "Words, Buildings, Machines," University of Virginia, Charlottesville, Virginia
     "The New Breed," University of Technology, Sydney, Australia

1989 "New York Architecture 1970–1990," Deutsches Architektur Museum,
     Frankfurt, Germany

1990 "Experimental Architecture: RIEA," AEDES Gallery, Berlin, Germany
     "Tokyo Forum Competition Entries," JAIA Building, Tokyo, Japan

1991 "Metropolis in Transition," Inspiration Gallery at the Axis Building, Tokyo, Japan

1992 "Caravan Project," Museum of Contemporary Art, Sydney, Australia
     "Furniture by Architects," Gallery of Functional Art, Santa Monica, California
     "Missing Link around Moscow," Inspiration Gallery at the Axis Building,
     Tokyo, Japan
     "The Future," Haus der Architektur, Graz, Austria

1997 "Space: AMA," Arlington Museum of Art, Arlington, Texas

1999 "Archilab," FRAC Center, Orleans, France

Selected Bibliography

Publications about Neil M. Denari

1986   MacNair, Andrew. "40 under 40." *Interiors* (September), 166.

1987   "StoreFront Architects." *Architecture + Urbanism* (Tokyo; February), 79–81.

1988   "The London Project." Exhibition catalog. New York: Princeton Architectural Press.

1989   Hogben, Gavin. "Young American Architects." *Architectural Review* (London; February), 51–53.
        New York Architecture 1970–1990. Exhibition book for the Deutsches Architektur Museum, Frankfurt. New York: Rizzoli.
        "Tokyo Forum Competition." *Shinkenchiku* (Tokyo; December), 202.

1990   "Projects." *Kenchiku Bunka* (Tokyo; February), 196.
        Miyake, Riichi. "Talk on House: Interview," *Kenchiku Bunka* (Tokyo, May), 27–29.
        Luschsinger, Christoph. "Los Angeles." *Werk, Bauen, + Wohnen* (Zurich), no. 7/8, 20–21.
        Nishimoto, Taeg. "Neil Denari: Interview and Projects." *Telescope* (Tokyo; Fall), 66–75.

1991   Betsky, Aaron. *Violated Perfection*. New York: Rizzoli.
        Cook, Peter, and Rosie Llewellyn-Jones. *New Spirit in Architecture*. New York: Rizzoli.
        Shane, Grahame. "Los Angeles Urbanism." *Architese* (Zurich; January/February), 75.

1992   Betsky, Aaron. "Young Los Angeles Architects." *Architecture + Urbanism* (Tokyo; June), 18–25.
        Betsky, Aaron, and John Chase, eds. *Experimental Architecture in Los Angeles*. New York: Rizzoli.
        Index Editors. *19 Approaches: Fenster Gallery Catalog*. Frankfurt.
        Muschamp, Herbert. " Reduced to Luxury." *New York Times Magazine*, 11 October, 32.

1993   "Central Glass Competition." *Shinkenchiku* (Tokyo; November), 290.
        Dollens, Dennis. "Eco-Tec in Corsica." *Telescope* (Tokyo; Spring), 46.
        "Birdhouses by Architects." *Architecture+Urbanism* (Tokyo; August), 14–19.
        Fuchigami, Masayuki. "Architect on the Scene." *Kenchiku Bunka* (Tokyo; May), 12.
        Henriksson, Stafan. "Neil M. Denari." *Magasin for Modern Arkitektur* (Stockholm), no. 4, 30–41.
        Zellner, Peter. "Discussion with Neil Denari." *Transition* (Melbourne), no. 41, 90–105.

1994   Dorrian, Mark. "The Recent Work of Neil Denari." *Artifice* (London: Bartlett Publication), no. 1, 9–24.
        Melet, Ed. "The Mysterious Architecture of Neil Denari." *de Architect* (Den Haag; October), 60–79.
        Ratterbury, Kester. Lecture review. *Building Design* (London; February), 14.

1995   Fuchigami, Masayuki. *51 World Architects*. Tokyo: Kenchiku Bunka Publications.
        "16hrs–Pacific Deployments: Neil M. Denari." Exhibition catalog from the Galleri ROM, Oslo.
        "Drawing Series Number 9," Toto Publications 1996 calendar, Tokyo.
        Fuchigami, Masayuki. *581 Architects of the World*. Tokyo: Toto Publications.

        Interview. *Columbia Newsline* (New York; January-February), 5.
        Martin, Elizabeth, ed. "Big Guitar." *Pamphlet Architecture #16*. New York: Princeton Architectural Press.
        "The Possibilities of the Computer in Architecture." *Space Design* (Tokyo; June), 46–49.

1996   Denari, Neil. "Interrupted Projections." *Architectural Profile* (Bangkok), no. 2., 76–81.
        Denari, Neil. "Interrupted Projections." *AD* (London), 33–37.
        "Interrupted Projections." *Shinkenchiku* (Tokyo; October), 22.
        Zellner, Peter. "Interrupted Projections." *The Interior* (Melbourne), 16.
        "Tokyo Prototype House." *JT* (Tokyo; December), 110–115.
        Lepore, Fabrizio. "Blob Fiction." *Ventre* (Milan), no. 4, 2–5.

1997   Codrington, Andrea. "Interrupted Projections at Gallery MA." *I.D.* (July-August), 147.
        Ourosoff, Nicolai. "Neil Denari." *Los Angeles Times*, 17 August, Opinion Section, 3.
        Zellner, Peter. "City of Sorts: Interview." *21C* (Melbourne), no. 24.

1998   Davidow, Joan, ed. *Space*. Arlington, Texas: Arlington Museum of Art Publications.
        "Casa Massey." *Architecti* (Lisbon), no. 42, 56–65.
        Zellner, Peter. *Pacific Edge*, New York: Rizzoli.

1999   Lopes, Diogo, ed., "Projects." *Prototypo* (Lisbon), no. 1.

Selected Writings by Neil M. Denari

1987   "The Contexts of the Machine." *Pamphlet Architecture* #12, Princeton Architectural Press.

1988   "Exploding Sonic Test Audio Visual Big Guitar." *Offramp*, SCI-Arc Journal no. 2, 18–20.
        "The Philosophy of Impossibility." The London Project exhibition catalog, Princeton Architectural Press.

1991   "Four Statements on Architecture." *Architecture + Urbanism* (Tokyo; March), 12–42.
        "Thoughts on Architecture and Education." *Kenchiku Bunka* (Tokyo; April), 154–155.

1992   "Arguments for Paralogical Geometries." *Oz* (Kansas State University), no. 14., 36–41.

1995   "Intransigent Desires." *Any* (New York), no. 10, 32–39.

1996   *Interrupted Projections*, Tokyo: Toto Publications.
        Recent Work, Bangkok: Bac/Esp Publications.

Credits

Data

First published in the United Kingdom in 1999
by Thames & Hudson Ltd, 181A High Holborn, London WC1V 7QX

First published in the United States of America in 1999
by Princeton Architectural Press, New York

British Library Cataloguing-in-Publication Data
A catalogue record for this book is available from the British Library

ISBN 0-500-28182-3

Printed and bound in Hong Kong

Design Richard Massey